Mind Gym

Emotional Intelligence, The Power of Silence, Mindset Mastery, Analyze People (Think Differently, Achieve More, Thrive, Mental Training)

Lance P. Richards

Mind Gym: Emotional Intelligence, The Power of Silence, Mindset Mastery, Analyze People (Think Differently, Achieve More, Thrive, Mental Training)

Table of Contents

Book 1 - Emotional Intelligence

Control Your Emotions and Eliminate Fear (Build Self Confidence, Boost Your Social Likability, Improve Interpersonal Connections, IQ, EQ)

1 - Introduction

I want to thank you and congratulate you for downloading the book Emotional Intelligence – Control Your Emotions and Eliminate Fear! By reading this book, you have taken the first step in learning to control your emotions and your life. Your journey toward building a stronger Emotional Intelligence and reaping the benefits of a healthier, fuller life starts now!

This book contains proven steps and strategies on how to become a truly empowered individual. Discovering the role that your emotions play in your life story will enable you to implement strategies to guide yourself to future success. Controlling your emotions and eliminating fear is all about taking the reins! This book will help you to identify negative emotions and learn to conquer them.

Here's an inescapable fact: you will need an understanding of Emotional Intelligence to make positive changes in your life. Emotions are powerful and complex. Research shows that Emotional Intelligence is everywhere.

If you struggle with social interaction, anxiety, stress, or even anger, you may need to take steps to improve your Emotional Intelligence. This book will help you to understand what Emotional Intelligence is, why it is important, and how you can use it to reach your goals.

Emotional Intelligence is both a gift and ability. Many lucky individuals are born with a naturally high Emotional Intelligence. We see many of these individuals in politics, the entertainment industry, and in leading positions in today's corporate business.

If you do not further develop your Emotional Intelligence, your entire life will be affected. Developing your Emotional Intelligence will give you powerful tools to navigate your professional, social, and private life. A high Emotional Intelligence strongly contributes to a happy, successful life story.

It's time for you to become an amazing individual! This book will help you to build your self-confidence, boost your social likeability, and improve your interpersonal connections.

We will explore the relationship between IQ (intelligence quotient) and EQ (emotional quotient) and how these factors influence your life. We will provide proven strategies to boosting your Emotional Intelligence, and provide your next steps in this journey. Congratulations, and good luck!

2 - What Is Emotional Intelligence?

Emotional Intelligence is a popular term in the media today: but what is it, exactly? This is a question Psychology researchers have been exploring for many years. Leading experts in Psychology and Neuroscience will confirm that there are many "types" of intelligence. You may have heard some individuals identify themselves as "book smart" or "street smart" or "money smart."

In simple terms, you can think of those with a high Emotional Intelligence as being "emotionally smart." Like any form of intelligence, some fortunate individuals are naturally gifted with high intelligence in some (or all) areas. The good news is that Emotional Intelligence is a type of intelligence that you can train!

With a little discipline and commitment, even those with a very low Emotional Intelligence can master the skills needed to become savvy, high-Emotional Intelligence individuals. Building your Emotional Intelligence can lead to the following practical benefits:

- Learning to recognize important emotional cues in others

- Learning to identify and respond appropriately to the triggers that trip your own negative patterns

- Learning to replace negative emotional patterns with positive ones

- Using your skills to navigate a social world

Emotional Intelligence is the unseen conductor that guides human interaction and society. Research has shown that those with a high Emotional Intelligence have gone on to reach success in both their private and professional lives. Those with a high Emotional Intelligence claim greater life satisfaction and stability than those of their peers.

High Emotional Intelligence individuals can include CEOs, Professors, Politicians, Gurus, and other public leaders. Research has shown a link between Emotional Intelligence and overall Intelligence (IQ): building a higher Emotional Intelligence will boost your IQ and lead to a happier, more successful life.

"Chapter 2: What is Emotional Intelligence" will begin by giving you the tools to understanding Emotional Intelligence and its role in your life. In this chapter, we will cover the two parts of Emotional Intelligence and important terms for understanding Emotional Intelligence.

Once we build your knowledge on what Emotional Intelligence actually is, we will proceed to Chapter 3, in which you will learn how Emotional Intelligence influences your life.

Later, we will help you to identify the emotional patterns in your life that you want to change and give you proven strategies for taking control. You will find practical advice for managing a variety of situations. Remember, every individual is different: use this book as a journey into yourself!

What are the two parts of Emotional Intelligence?

Emotional Intelligence is an elusive topic. Defining Emotional Intelligence is difficult because the subject is very broad. A quick internet search will have you confused and bewildered: there are too many opinions and ideas to gain a solid concept of Emotional Intelligence!

Luckily, scientists have been working on the question with peer-reviewed, trustworthy research. Professional investigation into emotional intelligence has narrowed down the subject into two specific parts:

"Trait" Emotional Intelligence

"Trait" Emotional Intelligence refers to the specific traits that contribute to your Emotional Intelligence. In thinking about Trait Emotional Intelligence, your personality and "born-with" traits come into play:

- Are you an introvert or an extrovert?

- Are you an optimist or a pessimist?

- Do you persevere or do you "give up"?

- Are you independent or codependent?

These aspects of your personality contribute to the ways in which you process and express emotions, which is an important part of your overall Emotional Intelligence.

Determining which personality traits contribute to your Emotional Intelligence is a complex process. Research shows that humans cannot be easily divided into groups or types: for example, you cannot definitively sort every individual into the labels of "introvert" and "extrovert." Humans fall along a continuum, with some being more extroverted or more introverted than others.

Your personality is formed by a combination of genetics and experiences. That is, researchers are unable to determine what parts of your personality were inherited, and which parts you learned through social interaction. This means that your behavior may change depending on the situation.

Some individuals may be introverted in the classroom, but come alive during a Friday night party. Others may be loud and outgoing in academic settings, but quiet and closed off in large social groups.

It is important to understand that your emotional reactions do not exist in a vacuum: the larger environment is always at play. Consider the following example:

A wife returns home from a bad day at work to find her husband with another woman. She is shocked and angry. She reacts by hitting this woman, breaking her nose. The woman is taken to the Emergency Room and presses charges against the wife for assault. The wife is arrested.

The wife in this situation lost control of her emotions and reacted in a way that was ultimately destructive to herself. When considering this situation, ask yourself:

- Did she lose control because of a personality trait,

like a bad temper?

- Was her control weakened by a bad day at work?

- Was she reacting to an intolerable situation?

- Did she naturally have an underdeveloped Emotional Intelligence?

The truth is, her response to the situation was probably influenced by all of these factors! Your Emotional Intelligence takes contributions from your genes, your life, and your current environment.

Researchers provide Trait Emotional Intelligence as a definition of Emotional Intelligence that is influenced by your genes and the environment in which you grew up and surround yourself with. Trait Emotional Intelligence is a combination of the following factors:

Temperament

Research shows that those with a more optimistic temperament are more likely to perceive events as positive, leading to a more appropriate and controlled emotional response.

Controlling Moods

Those with a high Emotional Intelligence are able to recognize and manage their moods with more skill than those with a lower Emotional Intelligence. Individuals with mood disorders especially have difficulty with identifying moods, regulating moods, and maintaining a positive outlook.

Interpretation and Coping Skills

Your personality is influenced by the way you interpret your environment. Those with an extroverted personality are more likely to interpret "bad luck" as a challenge, and cope more effectively. Effective coping skills lead to the cultivation of more positive emotions.

The personality traits most commonly linked with the influence of Emotional Intelligence are extroversion, introversion, and "neuroticism." Neuroticism is a term used by Psychologists to describe those who consistently exist in a negative mood state.

Those with neurosis are often anxious, frustrated, angry, sad, or depressed. Unsurprisingly, neurotic and introverted individuals seem to have the most difficult time measuring and regulating their mood, while extroverts seem to easily maintain a positive mood state.

Remember that Trait Emotional Intelligence is only one part of our quest to define Emotional Intelligence. As researchers and statisticians love to say, "correlation is not causation!"

This means that although a high Emotional Intelligence is correlated with those that are extroverted, it is still possible for an introvert to build and maintain a strong Emotional Intelligence. Understanding all sides of Emotional Intelligence is only the beginning!

"Ability" Emotional Intelligence

A second definition for Emotional Intelligence is known as "Ability" Emotional Intelligence. This is a new approach to the study of intelligence that proposes Emotional Intelligence as an additional form of intelligence.

As we discussed at the beginning of the chapter, there are many different "types" of intelligence. Researchers have formally identified Emotional Intelligence as a "type" of intelligence by defining "ability" Emotional Intelligence.

Researchers provide Ability Emotional Intelligence as a definition of Emotional Intelligence that is formed by your capacity for managing your emotions.

Research into general intelligence has shown that individuals have different "capacities" for critical thinking, verbal reasoning, spatial reasoning, quantitative reasoning, etc. Maintaining a high Emotional Intelligence may be representative of a higher capacity for managing emotions: thus, "Ability" Emotional Intelligence.

It is important to recognize that Ability Emotional Intelligence refers to a cognitive ability. This is different from the definition of Trait Emotional Intelligence in that an ability is not governed by your personality.

There are plenty of extroverts and introverts who show similar abilities in areas like math, science, and literature. Recognizing that Emotional Intelligence is, in part, an ability means that you can build your capacity for Emotional Intelligence: it is not simply something you are born with or born without.

The Emotional Quotient

Research shows that Emotional Intelligence is measurable

separately from general intelligence. Your general intelligence, or IQ, is a crude, general measure for clinically defined intelligence. The researchers that put forth the definition of Emotional Intelligence as an ability argue that Emotional Intelligence is a measurable cognitive ability.

Some are born with natural talent (Trait Emotional Intelligence), but everyone has to build and hone their Emotional Intelligence. The research argues that there is a Quotient, similar to the "Intelligence Quotient" (IQ) to measure Emotional Intelligence. They are calling this the "Emotional Quotient", or EQ.

Research has found that EQ has a close correlation with IQ: the higher your EQ, the higher your IQ tends to be. Your EQ is determined by how you perform on "Emotional Quotient" tests, just as an IQ is measured by your performance in "Intelligence Quotient" tests.

A low IQ measure is not always indicative of a low overall intelligence: thus, a low EQ measure is not always indicative of a low Emotional Intelligence. This means that EQ and Emotional Intelligence are not the same thing: the Emotional Quotient is a number that measures your Emotional Intelligence.

2 - WHAT IS EMOTIONAL INTELLIGENCE?

As you continue reading, remember that your Emotional Intelligence is affected by a variety of factors. When seeking to improve your own Emotional Intelligence, take time to reflect on your own life—your genetics, your life history, and your current situation—and consider how these factors may influence your Emotional Intelligence today.

3 - Emotional Intelligence in Your Daily Life

Now that you are well-versed in the two definitions of Emotional Intelligence, we can begin to explore the role that Emotional Intelligence plays in your daily life. Emotional Intelligence appears in the ways that you react to situations and the ways in which you interact with others.

Processing and managing your emotions has an effect on you and on the larger society around you. This means that Emotional Intelligence is at play everywhere, but particularly in your education, your career, your marriage, your social relationships, and even in the way that you handle emergencies.

Emotional Intelligence can be overwhelming, and it raises many questions. Some common questions include:

- If Emotional Intelligence is everywhere, how do I identify it?

- How do I know if I have a low Emotional Intelligence?

- How does Emotional Intelligence show up in my life?

Let's go through some specific situations and see if you can spot individuals who are acting with a high Emotional Intelligence, and individuals who are not. We will offer an explanation at the end for each scenario. We will offer examples of Emotional Intelligence in school, marriage, social interactions, and in dealing with fear.

Emotional Intelligence in School and Studies

Situation 1

Rachel is a college student. She has had a difficult semester: her boyfriend dumped her, she's living far from home, and she doesn't make much money at her job. Finals are approaching. Rachel is stressed, exhausted, and anxious. She can't sleep. The night before her big finals, Rachel goes out and parties with her roommate. The next day she is hungover and oversleeps. She fails the semester.

Situation 2

Stephanie is also a college student. It is her senior year! Her semester has been difficult: she had to take some extra classes to fulfill enough credits to graduate. Finals are approaching, and she wants to get to graduation! Her parents got divorced this semester and can't help her pay for bills.

She has been working many overtime hours to pay for a post-graduation vacation, but because of the divorce, she had to put that money into school. She is exhausted and stressed out about finals.

As finals week approaches, Stephanie knows that she is going to need time to study and to unwind, so she takes a week off of work. She takes time to calm down every night before bed so she can get a good night's sleep. She aces her finals and holds her head high at graduation!

Analysis

Which of these students displayed a developed Emotional Intelligence in making decisions? Rachel has had some hard luck: but instead of managing her bad moods and finding constructive ways to deal with her anxiety, she chose to use alcohol to calm down, and failed everything. By not managing her stress and frustration, she reacted in a very destructive way!

In contrast, Stephanie took steps to manage her stress, kept herself calm, and aced her tests. She recognized the emotions she was feeling and took the time to address them. Stephanie showed the traits of a person with a developed Emotional Intelligence, and this helped her to succeed in school.

Emotional Intelligence in Relationships and Marriage

Situation 1

Chris lives with his wife. He has been very caught up in work lately and hasn't been cleaning up around the house. His wife has been searching for a job and has been spending a lot of time at home. She has been doing all of the cleaning, as Chris has been too busy.

Chris has been very excited about his advancements at work and doesn't notice that his wife has been very quiet. He is surprised when, one night, his wife gets very angry at him, shouting that he never helps her with cleaning. Chris is unsure what he did wrong.

Situation 2

Andrew lives with his husband. He has recently been promoted at work, forcing him and his husband to move across the country. Andrew is used to moving and loves the new location, but his husband has never left home before and is homesick. Andrew's new position is taking off, but his husband is struggling to adapt and hasn't found a great job.

Andrew notices how frustrated his husband has been, and plans a special date for them to be together and talk it out. His husband admits his frustration, and he and Andrew come up with a plan to make things better. Both Andrew and his husband are satisfied that the new location is going to work out.

Analysis

Relationships are more complex for our emotions than handling personal challenges like studying for college finals. This is because there are now two individuals who need to act with Emotional Intelligence to make their situation work. Emotional Intelligence is not only about managing your own emotions: it is also about being in tune with the emotions of others, especially those closest to you.

In the first relationship situation, Chris seems to be an extrovert with a high ability for managing his own emotions. He is positive and excited and isn't experiencing any negative emotions or feelings. Unfortunately, Chris fails to notice that his wife is stressed out and frustrated. She has been having difficulty finding a job and has been cleaning up after both of them.

If she had managed her own emotions more efficiently, she could have brought Chris' attention to the problem and sought a solution. However, it seems that she bottled her emotions until she exploded!

On Chris' end, being more attuned to others' emotions should have tipped him off to the fact that something was bothering his wife: he was too excited to notice how quiet she had been! This situation could have been avoided by both parties.

In the second relationship situation, Andrew is also excited about the new changes in both his job and his location. His husband, however, is having a tough time. Andrew notices his husband's frustration and takes the time to address it. His husband manages his emotions well, and he has a civil conversation with Andrew about his difficulties. They are able to work it out and satisfy both parties.

These examples should show you that Emotional Intelligence in relationships is all about the interaction between two individuals. It is important to be in touch with both your emotions and those of your significant other.

The way that you handle your emotions and respond to those of your partner determines the way that you communicate. For an effective relationship, building and maintaining a high Emotional Intelligence is vitally important!

Emotional Intelligence: Social Interactions

Situation 1

Kelly is a shy person and feels awkward in social groups. She is outgoing only with her own group of friends. One day, her best friend invites her to go out with a group that she is unfamiliar with. Kelly agrees to go. She wants to be more adventurous. Once Kelly and her friend meet up with the group, her friend spends most of her time talking with someone else.

Kelly feels some jealousy but doesn't want it to ruin her night. She listens to the conversation among the other group members and notices that they are all laughing and enjoying themselves. One asks Kelly a question about work, and Kelly perceives her to be genuine and interested. Kelly starts to talk about her job, which helps to relax her. The rest of the night goes smoothly, and Kelly has made some new friends.

Situation 2

Jacob has always been a bit of an outcast. He works from home and has only a couple of friends. He tends to be very sarcastic and insists that people "don't get" his sense of humor. One night his friend is having a viewing party for a football game. Jacob comes along. Some of the guys are annoyed: their team is losing and they've put money on this game.

Jacob doesn't care for football. He feels uncomfortable around new people and cracks some sarcastic jokes at the expense of the losing team. The guys at the party start to dislike him. Jacob's friend is spending more time talking to a girl than to Jacob. Jacob feels more jealous and resentful as the night goes on and nobody talks to him. He leaves early in a frustrated mood.

Analysis

In the first situation, Kelly is shy, which would indicate that she feels some anxiety in new social situations. She recognizes that emotion but doesn't allow it to stop her, and agrees to go out with her friend. When Kelly feels jealous that her friend is not spending time with her, she solves the problem by listening and responding to the other individuals in the group.

She finds that by responding to their cues, she can carry a conversation and even make some new friends! Kelly is showing good control over her emotions. Her responses to her situation are indicative of a high Emotional Intelligence.

In the second situation, Jacob is also uncomfortable in new social situations. Unlike Kelly, he doesn't take the time to accurately read the people around him. If he had, he would have noticed that the guys watching the football game were upset, and maybe he would not have made jokes about their team.

The people watching the game were probably annoyed by Jacob and his jokes, and as Jacob became jealous of his friend, he became less pleasant to interact with. As a result, Jacob ends the evening frustrated.

Further along in the book, we will discuss strategies for navigating social situations similar to the examples given. It isn't always easy to read a room or to say the "right" thing, but we will give you foolproof, step-by-step instructions to get you started.

Emotional Intelligence: Dealing With Fear

Situation 1

Thomas has been having trouble with anxiety for several years. It began with social anxiety in high school and progressed until 30-year-old Thomas is almost completely housebound. New experiences worry him, and he is terrified of straying from his normal routine. He recognizes that his fear is irrational, and wants to change his life.

He wants to try to go to therapy but is scared of such a new experience. He decides to change slowly, every day. He adds something new to his routine each day as he builds his courage. At first, the changes are small; he will have something different for breakfast.

Eventually, he is brave enough to contact an online therapist. After several online sessions, Thomas is ready for referral to a therapist in-person. He is on the road to changing his life.

Situation 2

Lena is a teenager, and at the end of the school year, her friends are all going to an amusement park. Lena has always enjoyed spending time with her friends, but she has never been on a roller-coaster. She is scared. She gets more and more apprehensive as they approach the park, but she is terrified to mention her fear.

When they reach the park, her friends go straight to the biggest, fastest roller coaster there! Lena stands in line with them, too worried to tell her friends that she isn't sure about going on the ride. Her heart is pounding. She thinks she might faint. She thinks she might cry.

As she and her friends strap into the ride, she starts to cry uncontrollably and shrieks that she wants to get off. It's too late. The ride is already moving, and as it climbs the first hill, she can't stop crying. In 120 seconds, the ride is over, and she is laughing and smiling. It was fun!

Analysis

The first situation deals with an extreme case of fear. There are many individuals who develop minor anxiety and allow it to worsen until their situation is unbearable. Thomas showed a low Emotional Intelligence when he first let his anxiety get out of control. He mistakenly limited everything in his life, hoping it would solve his anxiety, but instead, he trapped himself in a routine.

Luckily, Thomas did develop a high enough Emotional Intelligence to recognize how irrational his behavior was. He took steps to alleviate his anxiety, and ultimately trained himself to work through his fear. He then sought professional help and continued to implement strategies to build his Emotional Intelligence, manage his fear, and continue on to a better life.

The second situation shows an individual who allows their fear to get out of hand and take over. Lena had many opportunities to identify her fear and communicate it to her friends. Her friends could have then helped her to work through her fear, either by convincing her the roller coaster was worth the anxiety, or by helping her to start with a smaller, more manageable ride.

When she didn't express herself, Lena found herself on the

most terrifying ride in the park! She allowed herself to be swept along, and because she did not address her fear, it only got worse. When she irrationally explodes and screams to be let off the ride, her anxiety has reached its peak. It is lucky for Lena that it was too late to leave the ride because she almost deprived herself of a very enjoyable experience!

These situations have highlighted just some of the major ways that Emotional Intelligence appears in our daily lives. Now that you have read some examples and seen Emotional Intelligence in action, consider the ways that Emotional Intelligence guides your life. As we've seen here, Emotional Intelligence is not always black and white.

There are some who make decisions based on a poor Emotional Intelligence, but work and build until they are acting with a stronger Emotional Intelligence. We have seen individuals who show Emotional Intelligence traits and individuals who cultivate Emotional Intelligence abilities.

In the next few chapters, we'll present step-by-step guides for recognizing your own Emotional Intelligence traits and building your own Emotional Intelligence abilities.

4 - Uncovering Negative Emotional Patterns

The first step in building your Emotional Intelligence is to identify the negative emotional patterns in your own life. You have seen how personality traits and situations affect our Emotional Intelligence and the ways in which we handle emotional situations. Now you need to consider the "don'ts" of Emotional Intelligence.

These are patterns that we want to eliminate from your life! Building Emotional Intelligence is about identifying and eliminating negative emotional patterns while simultaneously discovering and building positive emotional patterns.

By actively participating in this process, you will gradually learn to replace negative emotional patterns with positive ones. As you learn to assess and manage various emotional situations, you will build your Emotional Intelligence and journey on to lifelong success.

Common Negative Emotional Patterns

These are some generalized negative emotional patterns that seem to fall evenly across the human spectrum. These patterns are easy to adopt and difficult to lose. As you identify these patterns in your own life, try to consider why these patterns have evolved for you.

Avoiding negative feelings

One of the most common mistakes made by individuals who struggle with their Emotional Intelligence is to avoid recognizing negative feelings and emotions. This can lead to "bottling up" feelings and passive aggression and "explosions" later on. Yes, building your Emotional Intelligence is, in part, about trying to maintain a positive state of being.

However, this is not possible if you do not recognize the negative feelings that you have in certain situations and address them immediately. There is NO SHAME in experiencing emotion: even negative emotion! But you do need to recognize that emotion, address the source of that emotion, and decide on a solution to alleviating that emotion.

Spending time with those who maintain negative emotional patterns

There is nothing to be gained by surrounding yourself with individuals who actively seek or passively submit to negative emotional patterns. Peer pressure never ends, even in the adult world! Even if your friends or social group do not actively "pressure" you to behave with negative patterns, it is easy to emulate the people you spend your time with.

We are social creatures, and we adapt quickly to social situations. This means that we try to make ourselves as similar to our peers as possible: we may not even realize that we are doing so. Individuals who are not supportive of your quest to build a stronger Emotional Intelligence will only bring you down. They will encourage negative patterns in your life and make your journey that much more difficult.

Spending time on activities that trigger negative patterns

We all have to take out the trash at some point. Unless you're lucky enough to be able to maintain weekly house-cleaning help, you probably have to clean your house. We have to bring home a paycheck, we have to pay bills. These situations are unavoidable "necessities" to maintaining a life in today's society.

However, there are many areas of our lives that we have control over, even if we feel like we do not. Believe it or not, it is not necessary to pursue a career that you hate. If your job is causing you to fall into negative patterns, again and again, stop and assess.

Do you need to adjust your attitude about your position? Is there joy to be found in the position? If not, then you may need to consider moving on. Examine the activities in your daily life that bring you joy, and spend more time on those while you build your coping skills.

Negative self-talk

Putting yourself down is a common, destructive behavior that leads to negative emotional patterns. There is nothing to be gained by engaging in thoughts and feelings of worthlessness. Individuals with a high Emotional Intelligence are often associated with feelings of confidence. Building confidence can help you to build your Emotional Intelligence. Negative self-talk directly inhibits your progress.

Health Habits That Trigger Negative Emotional Patterns

Your health is important. Building a higher Emotional Intelligence can help you improve your overall health. In the same way, building a healthier body can help you achieve a higher Emotional Intelligence. It is important that you identify your health habits and how they may be affecting you and triggering negative emotional patterns in your daily life.

Avoiding Exercise

All of the medical, psychological, and social advice tells us that we MUST exercise. There is no denying the research that shows that regular exercise makes our lives better. Avoiding exercise is an avoidance behavior that leads to negative emotional patterns.

The less you exercise, the less healthy you are. Your entire body is a precious organism, and keeping the entire organism in optimal health is vital for mental health. Find a type of exercise you enjoy, and pursue it.

Regularly consuming unhealthy foods

Just as keeping your body healthy through exercise benefits your mental health, so does eating right. Consuming unhealthy foods worsens your health every time you eat. You build fat, bad cholesterol, and dehydrate your body. New research is showing that the delicate balance of your gut may play a critical role in your physiological and psychological health.

Consuming processed, artificial, sodium- and sugar-laden foods is a recipe for disaster for your gut. Eating bad simply makes you feel bad. Give your chances a boost by giving your body the fuel that it needs.

Regularly consuming alcohol or recreational drugs

You cannot, cannot maintain a healthy psychological and emotional state of being if there are chemicals in your system with the power to manipulate your thinking or your mood. Alcohol, for example, is a depressant, or a drug that suppresses your immune system and opens the door for negative emotional patterns.

Additionally, addiction is a very serious problem. Those who struggle with their Emotional Intelligence are more prone to addiction and should avoid any addictive drugs, especially while trying to analyze and address their own emotional patterns.

Encouraging addictive behaviors

Addiction is the word we use for becoming dependent on something. Clinically, addiction refers to a drug or a food: some kind of chemical that we put into our body that ignites reward pathways in the brain. Recent research shows that these same reward pathways are lit up by many different stimuli, ranging from sugar to sex.

If there is something in your life that you use as a crutch to get through the day, and you feel you can't live without it, you are encouraging addictive behaviors. Addictive behaviors are a part of a negative emotional pattern that evolves from being unable to face our own negative emotions.

We seek external stimuli to smooth over our negative feelings, and because those negative feelings were never properly addressed, they never truly go away. We continue using external stimuli to smooth over the issue because it is easy, but we fall into the trap of addiction.

Destructive Behavior and Thoughts

A big contributor to negative emotional patterns is destructive thoughts and behavior. Shame, anger, fear, and guilt are all deep thoughts that are difficult to suppress. They are not simple, situational emotions, and they contribute to our patterns of negative emotions.

Additionally, negative emotional patterns can feed into these destructive thoughts and lead to destructive behaviors. Try to identify some of the struggles you have had with these feelings, and examine what patterns and behaviors have contributed to them.

"It's not me it's you": Blaming others

It is easy to blame others for our own negative emotional patterns. Back in Chapter 3, we saw an example of a wife who ended up blaming her husband for the way that she was feeling. He hadn't properly noticed and interpreted her feelings. Rather than recognizing her role in the situation, she lashed out at him over the problem. It is difficult to identify our own faults.

It is a painful process. But as you look over your feelings and actions, remember that you are taking these steps to achieve future success. You are doing something wonderful for your own long-term health!

Recognizing your role in your negative emotional patterns

does not mean shifting blame to yourself and encouraging regret. You are simply identifying what actions contributed to the problem. You do not need to atone for these actions in any way: only try to find a solution so these actions do not occur again.

Dwelling on regret

Every human on the planet has made mistakes. If you are a person who is deeply empathetic or has made a mistake that you cannot fix, it often leads to destructive patterns of regret. Managing guilt is a difficult and arduous process.

The simple answer is to try to let go of the past: it is impossible to change it now, and you are on your way to better things! Often, getting rid of guilt and regret is not that simple. Try to identify the patterns of guilt and regret in your own life, and we will discuss solutions to this problem later in the book.

Encouraging fear through avoidance

Avoidance behaviors are often the result of psychological fear. You may feel anxiety about specific situations, or fear of feeling a certain emotion. The fact is, you cannot avoid your fear forever, and your life is not made better by doing so.

Do you remember the example in Chapter 3 that covered the man who allowed his life to be ruled by his anxiety? If you identify exactly what it is you are afraid of, you can begin to set goals and steps to manage and even eliminate that fear. Remember, everyone feels fear. How you respond to that fear is what will rule your life.

Regularly giving in to anger

Anger is possibly one of the most intense emotions. It can rise on a situational basis, or it can simmer for months or even years at a time. Anger is often intertwined with other negative emotional patterns: blaming others, addiction behaviors, avoidance behaviors, or even avoiding exercise.

Just like fear and guilt, anger can rule your life if you allow it to. Giving into anger is never acceptable, and in the long run, it is unhealthy for you. You must evaluate what is causing your anger, your role in that anger, and find ways to address your anger. We will discuss strategies for anger management later in the book.

Seeking retribution

Retribution-seeking is a destructive behavior that is closely related to anger and blaming behaviors. It is important to understand that seeking retribution is not an effective or acceptable way to ease negative feelings regarding an event or situation. Seeking retribution launches a negative pattern that allows you to justify acting in anger and blaming others for the way that you feel.

Perpetuating feelings of shame

Shame is feeling that you have done something inherently wrong that leads to humiliation, anxiety, and guilt. Shame in adult life is often brought on by feeling that society cannot accept you for who you are. Shame is closely intertwined with guilt and maintaining negative social relationships.

To alleviate shame, you must identify what causes you to feel ashamed. Have you done something wrong? Then see the section on guilt and remember, you cannot change the past. Are you surrounded by individuals who cannot accept you or refuse to forgive you? Then it is time to foster relationships with individuals who can love and accept you for who you are.

Identify Negative Patterns and Move Forward

This chapter helped you to identify some common behaviors that can lead to negative emotional patterns. Before beginning the next chapter, take some time to reflect on your own life. What behaviors have you engaged in that are perpetuating negative patterns? What role are you playing in your own negativity? Remember, you cannot solve a problem without first identifying the problem.

Chapter 5 will help you to identify positive behaviors that lead to positive emotional patterns. Many of these behaviors are directly opposite the negative behaviors presented in this chapter. You have identified the problem: now, let's identify what you do well.

5 - Discovering Positive Emotional Patterns

In Chapter 4, you saw a list of negative behaviors and the ways that these behaviors lead to negative emotional patterns. In this chapter, you will read about positive behaviors that lead to positive emotional patterns. Many of these positive behaviors are directly opposite the negative behaviors we discussed in Chapter 4.

As you find behaviors that you use in your own life and those that you do not consider replacing many of the negative behaviors mentioned in Chapter 4 with these positive behaviors. It will be difficult and doesn't happen overnight, but these two chapters are intended to present you with a contrast. These are the behaviors you want to encourage in your daily life.

Common Positive Emotional Patterns

These are some common positive emotional patterns that are seen in individuals that have a high Emotional Intelligence. These patterns encourage positive thinking and are indicative of good strategies for managing your emotions. Consider which of these positive emotional patterns already exist in your daily life, and which of these patterns contrast the negative emotional patterns that may exist in your life.

Acknowledging all feelings and emotions

It is important to acknowledge your emotions as you feel them. There is no such thing as a "bad" emotion: only negative patterns that stem from the ways in which you manage your emotions. Building positive emotional patterns starts with acknowledging your emotions. You should never suppress your feelings. It is okay to feel.

By acknowledging what and how you are feeling, you can then begin to process why you are feeling that way. Acknowledging your feelings enables you to begin examining your emotions objectively, so that you may start brainstorming solutions to negative patterns.

Individuals who possess a high Emotional Intelligence are often characterized by their ability to identify the emotions that they are feeling. Identifying and acknowledging your feelings is the first step to managing your emotions and an important part of building your Emotional Intelligence.

Surrounding yourself with supportive individuals

Having a support system is vital in any endeavor. The presence of a support system is so important, it is often considered a determining factor in whether a terminal patient will live or die, or whether a transplant patient thrives or deteriorates.

Supportive individuals can make or break relationships, careers, and huge life decisions. The common saying "it takes a village" is not only applicable to child-rearing! Spending time with individuals who love and support you will make all the difference as you strive to change your life.

Spending extra time on activities you enjoy

Taking the time to work on enjoyable activities has multiple benefits, from boosting feelings of wellness to boosting your overall self-esteem. Researchers have found that projects and sports are especially beneficial, as they give the participant the feeling that they have accomplished something.

It is important to take time for yourself and cultivate your own interests. In doing so, you build your self-awareness, an important part of Emotional Intelligence.

Learning to Love Yourself

Emotional Intelligence is all about knowing yourself, being able to recognize your emotions and accept them, and looking at your life with a constructive view. In order to achieve this, you must learn to love yourself. If you can love yourself, accepting all of your flaws, you can build confidence.

Confidence is the key to achieving a high self-esteem and ending anxiety in all spheres of your life. The following behavioral patterns will help you determine a pathway to developing a long-lasting relationship with yourself.

Being honest with yourself and with others

Research shows that holding on to secrets and lies can increase anxiety and deteriorate interpersonal relationships. "Being honest" doesn't mean that you have to share every mean thought or every dirty pleasure. Being honest with yourself is very similar to acknowledging your feelings. You are identifying yourself as a person, and acknowledging what makes you, you.

This is an important step in learning to love yourself, which is a huge step in ending fear and anxiety and building Emotional Intelligence. Being honest with others means that you cannot misrepresent yourself. Healthy social interaction does not thrive on lies.

Misrepresenting yourself or lying about your background and opinions can significantly increase your anxiety and self-doubt. In order to surround yourself with positive individuals, you must strive to be open and honest.

Positive self-talk

A second step in building your confidence and love for yourself is positive self-talk. Take the time each day to recognize the things that you have done well. Notice your small and large achievements and take the time to acknowledge and celebrate them.

Do not lie to yourself: simply accept and acknowledge the things that you have done well. Replacing negative self-talk with positive self-talk is a major life change with lifetime benefits.

Constructive Behaviors for Building Positive Emotion Patterns

Building constructive behaviors, or behaviors that serve a purpose in helping you to reach your goals, is another essential piece in building a high Emotional Intelligence. Those with a high Emotional Intelligence are able to act on their emotions after assessing them and come up with solutions to their emotional problems. Fostering constructive behaviors can aid you in this process.

Celebrating others' worth

Often, interpersonal communication problems arise because of deep-rooted jealousy issues harbored by those with a low self-esteem. Taking the time to acknowledge and celebrate the traits in others that you admire is a behavior that can help you to end jealous behaviors and celebrate your relationships with other people.

Remind yourself that others are people just like you: you only see what they want you to see, and many of them may be struggling with similar emotional problems that you are dealing with. Appreciating each individual for who they are will strengthen your interpersonal relationships and build your own self-esteem.

Actively bringing positivity into your train of thought

Building your Emotional Intelligence is all about changing the way that you think. You can actively encourage this process every day by paying attention to the thoughts that you engage in during the day.

Make a special point of noticing when negative thoughts cross your mind. When you are feeling negative about a situation, take the time to acknowledge that feeling and then bring a positive feeling into your train of thought.

For example, if you are thinking "It's such a gloomy day: I can't stand to go to work," then tell yourself that when you get home tonight, you can curl up with a fluffy blanket and a cup of tea. "Seeing the bright side" is an active process, and it will take some effort before it becomes natural.

Practicing forgiveness in your life

In Chapter 4, we discussed feelings of guilt and destructive behaviors like seeking retribution. Studies show that those who intentionally forgive others for wrongdoing are healthier, more positive individuals.

By forgiving others and moving on from situations that have caused you anxiety, anger, stress, or pain, you erase negative patterns from your life and encourage positive behaviors. It is important to actively, mentally forgive an individual, and deliberately put the situation behind you. You will reap psychological benefits from this difficult act.

Acknowledging your fears and facing them

As we discussed in Chapter 4, avoiding your fears gives you no opportunity to overcome them. To encourage positive emotional patterns, you must time the time to acknowledge your fears and find ways to face them.

This does not mean that if you are afraid of heights, you must go skydiving, but rather that if you are afraid of heights and it is interfering in your life, take heights in small, manageable doses until you can build up the courage to handle larger situations.

Perseverance

Above all, you must persevere in your behavioral changes.

Find little ways each day to acknowledge a negative emotional pattern in your life and replace the negative behavior with a positive one. There will be times that you are discouraged. Perhaps you chose to face a fear and it didn't work out: now you are more terrified than before! Setbacks happen.

You must be willing to understand that nothing works out right away! You will feel pushed back or even knocked down at times. It is okay to feel frustrated and angry. What is important is that you always maintain the will to try again.

Replace Negative Patterns With Positive Patterns

Now that you have an understanding of negative patterns and positive patterns, you can begin to identify these patterns in your life. As you move forward, take the time each day, possibly just before bed, to reflect on your day.

Think about the emotional situations that were presented to you throughout the day and how you responded to them. Try to identify the negative patterns and positive patterns that you see. As a guideline, consider the following questions:

- What negative emotional patterns or behaviors did you engage in today?

- How did these patterns affect your handling of emotional situations?

- How did these patterns affect your interpersonal relationships?

- What positive emotional patterns or behaviors did you engage in today?

- How did these patterns affect your handling of emotional situations?

- How did these patterns affect your interpersonal relationships?

- Did you replace any negative patterns with positive ones?

- What patterns are being repeated each day?

By considering these questions, you can assess your abilities in handling your emotions and keep a record of your progress. Remember, big changes start with small steps! No achievement is too small.

By finishing Chapter 4 and Chapter 5, you have learned to identify behaviors that contribute to your Emotional Intelligence. You are learning to replace negative patterns with positive ones. As you continue into the rest of the book, you will learn specific strategies for fostering positive emotional patterns, a vital step in improving your Emotional Intelligence.

6 - Strategies for Improving Your Emotional Intelligence

Now that you have learned what Emotional Intelligence is, how to identify its uses in your life, and how different emotional patterns contribute to your Emotional Intelligence, let's discuss daily activities that you can implement in your life to begin the process of improving your Emotional Intelligence.

First, we will discuss trademark "goals" set by researchers for those who are trying to improve their Emotional Intelligence. Then we will acknowledge conventional advice for lifestyle changes. Finally, you will learn situation-specific activities to help you navigate a social and emotional world.

Skills of a High Emotional Intelligence

When learning a new subject or pursuing a new goal, there are always specific goals that you set out to achieve. This book has focused on "Improving your Emotional Intelligence" and "Eliminating fear," but what specific skills should you seek to achieve in order to reach these lofty goals?

Researchers have targeted this exact question and come up

with some basic pillars of Emotional Intelligence that we will strive to build:

Self-Understanding and Awareness

- Recognizing emotions within yourself and identifying them accurately

- Recognizing your own strengths and weaknesses

- Building a strong self-esteem

- Accurately analyze your self-perception

Social Understanding and Navigation

- Building respect for others

- Fostering empathy for others

- Keeping your situation in perspective

Decision-making skills

- Identifying problems and assessing them objectively

- Critical thinking and problem solving

- Taking pride in ethical choices

- Self-reflection

Effective behavior management

- Managing stress and anxiety effectively

- Controlling impulses

- Fostering self-motivation

- Setting goals and enacting plans to achieve them

- Actively engaging in positive behaviors

Building Relationships

- Using clear and effective communication

- Learning to negotiate and cooperate with peers

- Encouraging others

These criteria for improving and measuring Emotional Intelligence are used by researchers across the country in building Emotional Intelligence in children and in adults. Take the time to study them and decide which of these criteria already apply to you, and which you need to work on. Keep these pillars in mind as we discuss strategies for improving your Emotional Intelligence.

Strategies for Building Self-Awareness

Building Self-Awareness is closely related to building your self-esteem and love for yourself. As you learn to respect and love yourself, it will be easier to analyze your emotions and your flaws and to develop strategies for managing them.

Keep a Journal

Monitoring your thoughts, emotions, and progress through writing is an effective way to self-analyze and begin managing your emotions. Journaling, whether on paper or computer, is an effective way to get your thoughts out in front of you so that you can perceive them in a different light.

Research shows that those that consistently journal often have a higher Emotional Intelligence than those that do not. Journaling can be used to let off steam, to acknowledge a feeling that you are having, or to reflect on your day.

Reading past journal entries will help you to monitor your progress on this journey. Consider starting a new journal to mark the beginning of your life change. You should:

Buy a new journal:

Seek a journal that encourages positive thinking. If bright colors give you a boost, look for a brightly-colored journal. If you enjoy posting an anonymous blog, start up a Tumblr or WordPress account.

Set aside a special time for journaling

This could be at breakfast, during your break at work, or even just before you go to bed. Pair journaling with something you look forward to (like a cup of tea before bed) so that you look forward to journaling each day.

Journal even if you don't feel like it

Journaling can have a way of turning your day around. Encouraging positive emotional patterns begins with taking tiny steps.

Engage in meditation.

Researchers have repeatedly shown that meditation is extremely beneficial to those who practice it regularly. Many people are unfamiliar with meditation and balk at this strange concept. Meditation does not mean that you have to sit cross-legged and chant for hours (though you certainly can if you want to). Meditation simply means taking time out of your day to do nothing else other than reflect. You should:

Eliminate Distractions

Meditation is about allowing your mind to wander freely. You cannot effectively meditate with the television blaring in the background.

Play Non-distracting Music

Soft, instrumental music can boost your brain activity and help the meditation process.

Take Deep Breaths

Breathe in deeply through your nose and out through your

mouth. You can be laying down, sitting straight, or even standing with your arms at your sides.

Let it go

Let everything go while you meditate. This is not a time to worry. It is simply a quiet time to allow your brain to relax. As with journaling, you should strive to make meditation a part of your routine. Choose a specific time of the day to meditate, and make it a priority.

Strategies for Managing Anxiety and Stress

Many individuals who are seeking to boost their Emotional Intelligence are dealing with significant anxiety and stress problems. Anxiety and stress are pervasive emotions that can grow if unchecked. To improve your Emotional Intelligence and build an awareness of these problems, these strategies may be helpful.

Make a plan to manage stress.

If you know that a stressful time is approaching, get organized. Write down important dates and deadlines and partition your work accordingly. Time management is a big part of stress management. Make a plan and stick to it! If this is new for you, try these steps:

Buy a planner with both monthly and weekly calendars. Visualizing your schedule can be an effective way to manage your stress.

Write down all deadlines and important dates in the planner. Use the monthly calendar to identify important dates.

Calculate your time effectively. How long do you have before your deadline? What do you need to complete before then?

Deliberately plan time for each day to get work done. Schedule this time in your planner! If you are a morning person, try to make time in the morning to get important work done. If you know you are exhausted after work, don't try to plan time right after work to complete your tasks! It will not get done.

Plan Rest Time

It is impossible to constantly work every hour of every day.

Your brain needs time to recharge, and you need time to relax and reflect. Set aside time every day to keep for yourself. Practice releasing your stress during this time. You can journal, meditate, do yoga, or participate in another activity that calms and focuses you.

Battle Anxiety With Action

When you are feeling anxious, your brain is feeling that something is wrong: an action must be taken. This often leads to negative behavioral patterns as you limit your activities to alleviate anxiety, or participate in senseless activities to calm yourself. Follow these steps to use positive, constructive action to battle your anxiety:

Identify the things that make you anxious

Are you worrying about an upcoming deadline? Perhaps there is something you can do now to contribute to your work for that deadline. If not, your anxiety may be irrational. Read on.

Find constructive activities that give you joy

Are you crafty, or a handyman? Do you have a pet that needs to be walked? When you start feeling anxious, actively engage in an activity that helps you to feel fulfilled.

Take away one piece of stress

Are you feeling generally anxious but know that you are stressed about the dishes in the sink? Take a few minutes to get them done. Taking away that one stressful factor may help to alleviate your anxiety.

Talk it out. Or you can write.

Talk to a close friend or relative about the way that you are feeling. Write about the way that you are feeling. Getting the problem in front of you can help you to analyze patterns and seek a solution.

Overwhelmed? Make one small change at a time

This book is full of steps and advice. It is easy to feel even more stressed and anxious when presented with lists and lists of steps and behavioral changes that you need to make. You may feel that you have no idea where to begin.

Find one thing—just one—that you know you can implement today. Once you have mastered that change, try another. This is a great way to gradually build confidence and maintain a long-term psychological change. Here are some ideas:

Commit to five minutes of self-reflection each day

Set a timer, and reflect, by journaling, meditating, taking a walk, or doing yoga. Five minutes is shorter than the average shower—you can reflect under the flow of hot water!

Add one healthy food to your diet

If you are struggling with what you eat, this is a great first step for change. Have an apple in the afternoon, or a side salad with your lunch or dinner.

Set your alarm for ten minutes earlier

Adding an extra ten minutes to your morning routine can give you room to "stretch" in the morning. If you typically feel that you are rushing to work, this extra ten minutes can give you valuable breathing room.

Strategies for Building Relationships

Emotional Intelligence isn't only about self-reflection and management. It is also about learning to read and respond to the individuals around you. You may be an individual who is flustered in social situations, or you may be having a hard time connecting to your significant other or to your children. The following are some general guidelines for building strong relationships with others.

Engage in active listening

When a person is talking to you, make a point of hearing them. Acknowledge that you aren't always going to be inter-ested in what they have to say, but recognize that what they are saying is important to them. To build a relationship, you need to make it important to you too.

Stop what you are doing

Try not to fidget or engage in other activities, like watching television, while someone is talking to you. Rote memory tasks like washing dishes or driving usually afford your mind enough space to listen effectively.

Try to make eye contact

If you are driving, this is a bad idea. But if you are at dinner or at work or attending a get-together, making eye contact can help keep you focused on the person who is speaking, preventing your mind from wandering.

Truly consider what the person is saying

Remain objective. A good way to do this is to mentally repeat the words that you hear and come up with questions to further clarify the speaker's intent.

Communicate clearly and honestly

When responding to another person, practice being honest without being offensive. Plainly state what you are thinking, and do not pretend to know facts or have opinions that you do not.

Do

Ask questions

After assessing the topic the speaker is discussing, ask questions to help you with clarification and furthering the conversation. Avoid yes/no questions. Some examples include:

- "How did you get into the business?"

- "I'd like to know more about this subject. Can you point me to some resources?"

- "How long have you been feeling this way?"

Remain honest

If you have no previous experience with a subject, say so, and follow up with a question. This shows that you are interested in learning more.

Remain patient

Conversations are about cooperation between two or more people. You may feel a burning need to say something, but take the time to listen. This will help you effectively "read the room" and respond appropriately to others. Wait before speaking.

Remain open to learning

Don't

Interrupt

Never, ever interrupt, unless you desperately need to leave or are about to have a serious bathroom emergency. Interruption is rude and disrespectful.

Use offensive language

Fostering relationships is about building a bridge. Using offensive language or blatantly stating controversial opinions can burn that bridge quickly.

Ask yes/no questions

These questions limit responses to one word, and one-word conversations get dull quickly.

Spend time and effort on others

Doing things for the people in your life is a wonderful way to show affection, commitment to the relationship, and respect for other individuals. If your wife is exhausted after dinner, take the time to do the dishes, and maybe go the extra mile to make her a cup of tea.

Make plans to do little things for other people. Treat your best friend to coffee, or buy your new coworker breakfast to welcome them to the team. Bringing a little joy to someone else's life will almost always bring joy to yours. Just remember that kindness is only kindness with no strings attached: do not expect repayment or overwhelming gratitude. Simply do.

Consider the feelings of others

Recognizing that others feel and think in similar ways to you is a major step in building cooperative relationships. Developing empathy is vital to maintaining your relationships. Here are some guidelines to help you navigate your relationships with others:

Make a note of the little things

Is your husband quieter than usual? Does your coworker

seem sad on Thursdays? Has your boss been taking a lot of sick leave?

Watch facial expressions

When communicating with others, make a point of looking them in the face (preferably making eye contact). Pay attention to their expressions when they are happy, sad, or angry. With time, you will begin to read facial expressions before any spoken communication, and be able to respond appropriately.

Put yourself in their shoes

Did your coworker work a double today? They are probably tired. Is your girlfriend having trouble coming up with rent? She is probably stressed.

Pay attention to patterns

If your significant other is always exhausted on Fridays, consider planning something special on Fridays. Even an action as simple as ordering a pizza each Friday can be a fun and rewarding activity.

Building relationships is about perceiving and responding, perceiving and responding. As with anything else, the more you practice, the more skilled you will become at understanding how to recognize emotional cues from others.

Maintaining strong relationships will be easier as you learn to efficiently interpret actions and expressions. Responding appropriately is a major benefit of improving your Emotional Intelligence, and you will watch your relationships flourish!

Implementing Strategies in Your Own Life

Now that you have read about different strategies for building different aspects of your Emotional Intelligence, it is time for you to actively implement them. The strategies presented are applicable to a variety of situations, and though they target certain emotions or circumstances, they will assist in improving your overall Emotional Intelligence.

As you continue to grow and learn, use the resources available to you to build on your experience. If yoga helps you manage and contain your emotions, and you are also seeking social interaction, join a yoga studio! The advice of others who are more practiced in the field will benefit you enormously.

Use the internet to find communities and forums for support if you aren't ready for face-to-face social interaction yet. Even if you are, the internet can be a valuable resource. You can find additional advice to supplement what you have already learned from this book. You must be your own coach once you finish this book and move on.

The next few chapters will specifically target difficult obstacles in developing your Emotional Intelligence. Read on to discover how to manage anger and eliminate fear.

7 - Obstacles: Anger and Fear

Fear and anger are some of the most powerful emotions that you will encounter in your life. They often occur in the moment, and can feel insurmountable. When people react strongly in different life situations, they are often motivated by fear, anger, or both. Fear and anger seem to hijack your sense of reason and cause you to act without thinking.

Research has found that emotions like fear and anger are closely linked with our built-in "fight-or-flight" response. When you feel something as strongly as fear or anger, your adrenaline starts moving, and your fight-or-flight response is kicked into high gear. Your body starts pumping more blood and oxygen to your muscles, and the decision-making center of your brain slows down.

This is because fight-or-flight situations call for you to react quickly, without thinking a situation through. This is a good thing if you are being mugged: it is a bad think if you are responding to an everyday life situation. This chapter will focus on calming your fight-or-flight mode on a situational basis as well as provide strategies for dealing with longer-term fear or anger.

Dealing With Situational Anger

Everyone will encounter a situation that makes them angry. Life is frustrating and unfair, and you will encounter other humans who seem determined to make your situation difficult. Before we begin discussing steps for managing your anger on a situational basis, let's discuss some common causes of anger.

What makes you angry?

There are common reasons for everyone to get angry. The following list includes situations or feelings that often lead to intense or even violent anger. If you struggle with anger, consider the following list and think about what often seems to make you angry. Identifying your triggers is a vital step in learning to manage them.

Unfair Situations

It is easy to get angry when you or someone close to you has been treated unfairly.

Feeling Powerless

Unfair situations can often lead to feelings of powerlessness. Being unable to act can cause mental stress and lead to anger.

Responding to Provocation

We often become angry in our interactions with other people or with animals. There are several kinds of provocation that can lead to anger.

Insults

Getting insulted is a type of provocation. We often feel that we must respond to an insult. This behavior is observed by researchers in humans and in animals: we seem to need to defend our honor, or pride, by responding angrily to insults.

Physical Contact

Physical contact is a form of provocation. When another human or animal physically attacks you without invitation, your body can respond by quickly throwing you into fight-or-flight mode.

Increasing Stress

Feelings or stress or frustration that aren't addressed can

quickly lead to a flare-up of anger.

Is it ever "okay" to react with anger?

The short answer is no. Anger is an emotion that induces your fight-or-flight response, dampening the processes in the executive decision-making area of your brain. Responding with anger will always mean that you are responding without sufficient thought behind your actions.

Improving your Emotional Intelligence means becoming a person who always considers before acting. Reacting with anger makes this impossible.

Strategies For Managing Your Anger

Recognize your anger

When your anger first flares, you won't be focusing on you, but the object of your anger. Take a moment to realize that you are angry.

Take deep breaths

You are angry. Your body is in 100% fight-or-flight mode. You need to tell your body that this is not a fight-or-flight situation. Breathing slowly and deeply through your nose and out your mouth will slow your heart rate and decrease the flow of adrenaline.

Remove yourself from the situation

If you just can't stay in the room without hitting the guy who just made a rude comment to you, leave. As you learn to manage your anger, you will gradually be able to remain calm while staying in a situation. It is better to leave and calm down than to react.

Take it out somewhere else

When we feel angry, our body feels the need to act. Sometimes calming your heart rate is not enough: your body is ready to go and wants to act. Physical activity is usually most helpful with this. Go to the gym or buy a punching bag.

Engage in "cathartic" activities

Singing loudly to your favorite song blaring through your car stereo, or using art to express your feelings are great ways to get the anger out without getting physical.

Anger That Festers

Sometimes anger is not a quick flare-up that you have to deal with in one situation. Some events can leave you with feelings of anger for months or even years. Someone may have wronged you, you may have fallen on some hard luck, or you may not even have a reason for your anger.

This kind of anger can slowly eat away at your life, making relationships, social interaction, and career success extremely difficult. Your mind focuses and obsesses over your anger, blocking out everything else.

Strategies

Identify negative emotional patterns

Chapter 4 identified some negative emotional and behavioral patterns that result from feelings of anger. Take the time to identify these patterns and try to replace them with positive patterns.

Retribution seeking

This is a negative behavioral pattern. You may feel that you have been wronged and cannot rest until retribution is paid. Research has found that revenge rarely alleviates our frustration, and sometimes can even make our negative feelings worse. Recognize that this is a negative pattern and will only harm you.

Blaming Behaviors

Like retribution-seeking, assigning blame is not productive. You are seeking to manage your anger, and you must recognize your role. You cannot do this if you are intent on blaming others for your situation.

Accept your situation

Blaming others and seeking retribution are not going to change the situation that made you angry. You must accept the situation so that you can take productive steps to improving it.

Get some perspective

When you are constantly feeling angry with your life, it can be helpful to get some perspective. Try volunteering at a soup kitchen or a homeless shelter. Helping others is a great way to make yourself feel better, and a wonderful way to gain some perspective on your life.

Do Not Allow Anger to Rule Your Life!

Anger is a corrosive emotional pattern that must be addressed and rectified. Living your life in anger is not healthy, and research shows that feelings of anger are associated with elevated cortisol levels. Cortisol, also known as the "stress hormone" has well-known negative effects on your health and well being.

Cortisol limits your ability to sleep, to process emotion, and impairs your long-term cognitive ability. If you are struggling with anger, you must take steps immediately to relieve it. If you are planning to implement one small behavioral change at a time to improve your Emotional Intelligence, begin with anger.

Dealing With Fear

Like anger, fear can be situational, or it can be long-term. Long-term fear is usually identified as anxiety or a phobia. Fear can impair every aspect of your life. It can interfere with social interactions, relationships, or your career. Left alone, fear will only grow.

It is a paralyzing monster that can strangle your life! As you identify strategies for managing fear, consider what you are afraid of. Unlike anger, fear does not always fall under a blanket of "common" causes. Fears range from phobias of spiders to a fear of getting intimate with another person. Before you continue reading, reflect on what you are afraid of in your own life. Consider the following questions:

- How does your fear show up in your daily life?

- Are you afraid regularly (more than 1-2 days a week)?

- What causes you to feel afraid?

- Does your fear affect your social life?

- Does your fear affect your relationships?

- Does your fear affect your career?

- Are you hiding from your fear?

The following strategies will help you to manage fear, both situational and long-term, in your daily life.

Strategies for managing situational fear

Take deep breaths

Just like anger, your fear is stimulating your fight-or-flight response. Deep breaths will help to counteract this response and enable you to think clearly.

Assess the situation

Again, there are many reasons to be afraid. The first question you must ask yourself is: Is your life or another's in danger? If not, consider any safety risks to yourself.

Be honest with yourself

What is the worst thing that could plausibly happen in this situation? By "plausibly" we mean that freak accidents (a roller coaster running off the tracks or a plane crashing) are unlikely to occur.

Assess your needs

If your life or another's life is truly in danger, you need to consider all possibilities for removing yourself from the situation. If not, consider whether you need to leave the situation or not. Will the situation benefit you in some way? For example, if you are flying to Paris but are afraid of flying, your "need" is to get to Paris.

Take action

Take every step you need to either remove yourself from the

situation or eliminate your fear. If you are on a plane and afraid of flying, use noise-cancellation headphones to block out your surroundings. If you are about to get on a roller coaster and decide you are much too afraid, leave the situation.

Situational fear is tricky and can be frustrating. If you know that you will be in a situation that will engage your fear, plan ahead. Bring noise-cancellation headphones to your flight. Take steps to help yourself.

Strategies For Managing Long-term Fear

Managing long-term fear is similar to managing situational fear. You must identify what you are afraid of. Plan ahead for situations that will cause you fear. Take deep breaths when fear comes on. Assess situations of fear and take to help yourself. For behavioral and emotional strategies for managing fear and anxiety, see Chapter 5.

You can also handle your long-term fear by talking to someone: a friend, family member, even an online forum. Getting your fear out and getting advice from others in similar situations is a great way to start managing fear. Like anger, fear is crippling.

Addressing it is vitally important! All of the steps for improving your Emotional Intelligence will help you to manage your fear as well. Building confidence, interpersonal relationships, and remaining calm are all remedies for fear in your life.

Moving On

Now that you have built an understanding of Emotional Intelligence and its role in your life, as well as addressed specific emotions and ways to manage them, it is time for you to decide what you want and reach for it. Use the strategies provided in this book to boost your confidence and self-awareness.

Do not let fear or anger hold you back! You are in control. You have taken the reins of your life and it is time for you to move on to bigger and better things. You are unstoppable, and it is time for you to blossom!

8 - Conclusion

Thank you again for purchasing this book!

I hope this book was able to help you to build your Emotional Intelligence and take control of your own life.

The next step is to implement positive behavioral changes, find the strategies that work for you and further explore specific methods that apply to your situation. Improving your Emotional Intelligence is an exciting, lifelong journey. You are well on your way. Congratulations on taking this step into self-discovery!

Thank you and good luck!

Book 2 - The Power of Silence

Winning The Battle Over The Noise Of Life (Inner Life, Introversion, Busy Life, Power Of Quiet, Slowing Down)

1 - Introduction

Do you constantly find yourself stressed out, tired, or overwhelmed? Do you want to step away from the noise of life? Are you looking for simple yet effective strategies to attain rest and relaxation?

If so, then this book definitely has what you are looking for!

This book will share with you the reasons why silence can be the most effective way towards attaining peace of mind and clarity of thought. More importantly, you will find here the strategies that will let you make the most of these quiet times of solitude.

You can also expect to find practical solutions on how to understand your inner self, create your quiet space, and simplify your daily life. Aside from these, you will also learn how to develop habits that you can thoroughly enjoy in the midst of peaceful and silent solitude, including a digital detox, journaling, meditating, connecting with nature, and reading for pleasure.

This book is dedicated to those who want to break free from the daily grind, those who wish to discover the more hidden aspects of themselves, and those who simply want to appreciate life in the present moment.

Begin your journey towards discovering the power of silence now. So, without further ado, onto chapter 2.

2 - The Power of Silence

"True silence is the rest of the mind, and is to the spirit what sleep is to the body, nourishment, and refreshment."

William Penn

The modern world has become filled with so much more stimuli than it ever did before, especially now with all the latest advancements. Every which way we turn, there always seems to be something going on that we often times could not help but try to become a part of it.

For instance, we have instant chat messaging to communicate with everyone from our next-door neighbor to our friends from across the globe, when back then we had to wait for weeks before receiving a reply. Libraries might not even be as popular nowadays because we can now save thousands of books and other sources of information within a palm-sized device.

Back then, people also had to visit the public library and scour through shelves upon shelves to find the reference they are looking for. Now, it takes a few seconds for anyone to find answers to most of their questions because of search engines like Google.

Of course, we must be thankful for all of these amazing inventions because they have made life much more convenient, to say the least. They have helped a lot of people broaden their knowledge and skills, got people together into one platform without leaving their homes so as to discuss and collaborate on innovations, and they have millions of ways to entertain us and help us escape from the humdrum of routine.

The problem only starts when we become so wrapped up in the activity and noise of our world that we fail to appreciate the other aspect of our lives: silence.

When people talk about silence, they usually refer to the absence of sound. Silence is a word most people usually associate with libraries and other really "strict" institutions because it discourages people from talking to each other and being a disturbance.

Silence is also a way of protesting, of refusing to speak even when expected to. When we are angry or disappointed, silence is sometimes the preferred way to show how we feel without really saying anything.

As you can see, silence has many meanings. In this book,

however, it refers to freedom from noise and agitation, from disturbances, stress, and intense emotions.

To be in a place of quiet means to be in a place where much input – the opinions of other people, auditory experiences such as music blasting from one's earphones, the pressures of the workplace – cannot penetrate into your mind. It is a time when you have enough energy and space to enter into a deep state of thought.

To inspire you to have more moments of stillness, peace and quiet, here are some of the benefits you can gain from the power of silence:

It is good for our mind.

Our everyday lives are now bombarded with so much sensory input that the World Health Organization has even referred to it as a "modern plague" that negatively affects one's health. Indeed, many of us have become so used to always listening to music, watching videos online, and practically overloading our senses with stimuli, that we are inadvertently triggering unnecessary stress and tension.

Moments of silence, on the other hand, can help the brain the brain restore itself. It fact, silence may be more effective at stabilizing blood circulation than relaxing sounds, according to a study published in the April 2006 issue of the journal Heart.

Another study, published in the December 2013 issue of Brain Structure and Function, reveals that silence can help the brain regenerate new cells in its hippocampus or the region linked to our memory, emotions, and ability to learn.

It helps us tap our inner self.

Our inner self can be defined in many terms, depending on what their motive is, but in this particular book, it simply refers to the stream of ideas, thoughts, emotions, and memories that flow in your mind and that you can witness and understand better without the distractions of the outside world. The only way to really engage with our inner self is by eliminating distractions and entering the state of silence.

The advantages to tapping our inner self are plentiful. For one, it helps you unleash your creativity. People widely known for their intelligence and creativity such as Albert Einstein, Alexander Graham Bell, Lewis Carroll, and T.S. Eliot, have praised the effects of solitude and silence on their thinking process, and they give it part of the credit for what they have created.

It brings to light our unhealthy habits.

Have there been times when you swear to quit a bad habit, only to find yourself being hooked to it more than ever? Or maybe you believe yourself to be stuck in an unhealthy relationship with someone, but it is somehow challenging for you to stop communicating with that person or making excuses for their behavior.

Whatever your unhealthy habits may be, you can only recognize them for what they truly are and how much damage they have caused in your life if you spend some time in silent thought.

The beauty in this, though, is that you will also be able to see the most effective means by which you can overcome these unhealthy habits. Naturally, it won't make the transition easier, but you will be able to solve your problems better.

It helps us put things into perspective.

Picture a fresh graduate who wants to start her own company and has decided to work for a company from which she wants to learn the ropes and earn enough for her start-up capital at the same time.

Along the way, she encounters so much gossip, idea stealing, and "politicking" among her peers and so many crazy demands and fits of anger from her boss that she decides to put in less effort, clock in fewer hours, and even join in on the power play. In the process, she began to lose sight of what she originally aspired for – the dream business she had been dreaming of right when she graduated from college.

You have probably experienced many hiccups in the daily grind yourself, and it might have caused you to let go of certain aspirations in your life. Indeed, there are times when we feel so overcome by difficulties that we would go so far as to contemplate quitting.

However, if we try to disengage from the throes caused by failure and tribulations and through silence consider our reasons behind the struggle, we will be able to rekindle our passion towards the goal we wish to achieve.

It reminds us of what is important.

Have you ever encountered a little exercise wherein you are asked to imagine yourself in your own wake, surrounded by the people whom you believe would visit you at your funeral? If you have not, then you might like to give it a try. If you have, then it would still be a good idea to try it again as a gentle reminder. Here is how you can do it:

Find a cool, quiet and dim place where you can lie down undisturbed for a few minutes. Once you are there, go ahead and lie down comfortably. Close your eyes. Now, imagine that you are in a wake, your wake. All the people you know have been informed of your passing.

In your mind's eye, visualize who the people in your wake are. Can you find the ones who matter the most to you? How are they coping with you being gone? Lay silently as you imagine each person and what they would say about you, or even what they are thinking as they gaze at your lifeless body.

Now, spend some time looking back on how you lived your life up until today. Would you say you had lived it free from regrets? If you do have some regrets, what are they and why

do you regret them

consider them to regret? If you still had the opportunity to go back and fix them, would you? How would you go about it?

Try not to rush through this experience, because you would be able to commune with your mind in such a way that it cannot be replicated in any other situation. Allow your thoughts to flow freely, and if a particular thought stirs up your emotions, let yourself express these feelings as well.

This is the beauty of silence, as it allows you to call forth your deep-seated thoughts and then, hopefully, spark you to pursue the things that you might regret if you had not.

Naturally, you would be able to have more unique experiences and enjoy personal benefits from the power of silence. Of course, the only way to find out what these could be is to practice having moments of quiet every day.

The rest of this book will give you plenty of tips and ideas on how, through silence, you can learn more about your thoughts, emotions and unleash your mind's full potential, and win the battle against the noise of life.

3 - Understanding your Inner Self

"There is an amazing power getting to know your inner self and learning how to use it and not fight with the world. If you know what makes you happy, your personality, interests, and capabilities, just use them, and everything else flows beautifully."

Juhi Chawla

Are you an Introvert or Extrovert?

Do you like to read books or articles about psychology or personality types? Those who do are most likely familiar with the concepts of introversion and extroversion. However, if you are unsure of whether you are an introvert or extrovert, you can try answering the following questions with a yes or no:

- You have been told you are a good listener.

- You are fond of writing your thoughts out on paper more than you do talking about them to a friend.

- You tend to spend more time conversing with just one person than with a group of people.

- You like spending time alone.

- You prefer to discuss deeply about topics that are important to you than to make small talk.

- You do not like getting into arguments with other people so you prefer to keep quiet when you are upset.

- You like doing work yourself than collaborating with others.

- You have been described as quiet or soft-spoken for more than once in your life.

- Your idea of a happy celebration is experiencing it with close family and/or friends instead of a large group.

- You do not find it difficult to focus on a task for an extended period of time.

- When someone calls you, you sometimes tend to let it go through to voice mail or consider not answering and then just texting them afterwards.

- After a day out in public such as when you go shopping, you come home feeling tired even if you did enjoy the activity.

- You like to take your time thinking about how to respond to something before you say your thoughts aloud.

- You are disinclined to share your opinions, achievements, and/or life's moments on social media.

- You would rather not discuss or reveal your work to your peers until you have completed it.

So, now that you have answered all of these statements, count how many times you said "yes." If out of 15 statements at least 10 of your answers are yes, then you are more of an introvert.

The reverse is true if at least 10 are no. If your answers are a roughly equal distribution of yes and no, then you may be able to call yourself an ambivert – or someone who is inclined to be introverted in an equal number of situations as he/she is extroverted.

Some people think introverts are the shy ones and extroverts are the loud ones, but that is actually not the way it works. Rather, you can tell whether you are an introvert or an extrovert based on how you restore your energy.

On one end of the spectrum, extroverts feel happier, stronger, and more energized when they spend time with other people, which means they tend to lose energy when they are alone.

Introverts are the exact opposite, in that they gain energy and happiness when they are in solitude, and their energy is depleted when they socialize, especially with large groups of people.

Take note that introversion should not be mistaken for shyness, or the fear of being embarrassed because there are plenty of confident introverts who do not hesitate to engage in an animated conversation with strangers if it is a topic that means a lot to them.

Also, some extroverts happen to be shy, and this proves to be a difficult situation for them because, despite their constant need for companionship, their shyness keeps them from approaching others.

The reason why it is so important for people to know whether they is an introvert or an extrovert is so they can understand why they feel or act in a certain way during specific situations. For instance, introverts who are unaware of their nature could suffer in silence for years in a society biased towards extroverts.

Do you currently have a Fixed or Growth Mindset?

Have you ever heard of the concept "fixed and growth mindset?" It was discovered by a psychology professor named Carol S. Dweck, who discussed this in detail in her 2006 book Mindset: The New Psychology of Success. But before we talk about that, you can answer the following questions to determine whether the way your mindset works right now is leaning towards the fixed or the growth kind.

It is best to have a pen and paper ready. To answer these statements, write 4 for "completely agree," 3 for "agree," 2 D "disagree," and 1 for "completely disagree."

- I am at a certain level of intelligence that I cannot really do much about.

- My intelligence is who I am.

- Not everyone can become smart no matter how hard they try.

- Each of us is born with a set of talents.

- It is always stressful when you are trying out new things.

- Some people are born kind, and some are born cruel. That's how the world works.

- Feedback from other people is hard to accept.

- Smart people do not have to try as hard as the not so smart ones to get good grades at school.

- It is important to look smart all the time so people will respect you.

- You think it is hard to lose weight and not everyone is capable of doing it.

After that, you have given your answer to these statements. You can go ahead and total your score. If your score is between 31 and 40, then you are likely to have a fixed mindset right now.

If it is between 21 and 30 then it means most of your ideas could be fixed, but not all. If you got between 11 and 20 then you probably have an equal number of fixed and growth mindset-based ideas. But if it is 10, then you are likely to have a growth mindset.

Now, take note that this test should never define who you are because there are not enough statements and scenarios to really help you dig deeper into your inner self, as far as your mindset goes. However, it does serve as a "peek" into the way your mindset works. That said, let us now talk about the difference between a "fixed" versus a "growth" mindset.

Carol Dweck describes the fixed and growth mindsets in relation to learners. She said that learners or students who have a fixed mindset are those who think that their intelligence, talents, and abilities are fixed traits.

Specifically, they believe they have a certain amount of these traits and that there is nothing they could do about it. Also, the goal of those who have a fixed mindset is to always look smart to others and to avoid looking stupid.

On the other side of the spectrum are the learners with a growth mindset, who believe that they can develop their intelligence, talents, and abilities as long as they put in the effort, are persistent, and have good teachers. While most of them do not think everyone can become like "Einstein," they do think they can "get smarter" as long as they try hard enough.

In a nutshell, those with the fixed mindset believe everything is set or fixed. Those with the growth mindset, on the other hand, believe they can continue to grow if they so try. It is so important for anyone to know which of the two mindsets their inner self is feeding because then they would be able to do something about it.

In fact, by believing that you can do something about, you are already starting to think in the growth mindset way. With the help of introspection and the power of silence, you can take the time to listen to how your inner self-perceives itself and the world as well as responds to situations.

Developing the growth mindset and diminishing fixed ideas will enable you to achieve anything you want. It will dramatically boost your self-confidence and also help you become more optimistic towards your goals and abilities.

You will also be able to help other people who are still struggling with a fixed mindset because then you could explain to them that they can be smarter, more creative, stronger, faster, more intelligent, and successful if they focus on improving themselves constantly.

What are your Values in Life?

Your values are basically your beliefs in which you are emotionally invested, which means you hold them with utmost importance. Whatever we encounter that is not in line with our values, we reject. However, if we are thrust into a situation in which we cannot say no to whatever is not in line with them, then our lives would become miserable.

For example, let us say your relationship with your family is your number one value. Yet, due to your long work hours, you could barely spend time with them. As a result, your work makes you feel miserable and your mind and body both suffer from the seemingly relentless stress.

The only way to overcome this is to reaffirm your values – or the importance of your family to you and the time to spend with them – so you can make adjustments to your life choices (maybe not taking on so much work or even considering another job?) so that you can live the life you truly want.

As you can see, knowing exactly what your values are will

enable you to understand why you make decisions the way you do and live the kind of lifestyle you have. Also, it is important to remember that our values may change over time depending on the experiences we have throughout our lives. Therefore, we should check on our values every so often.

With all these in mind, here are the guidelines that may help you identify the values deep within your inner self. It is best to reflect on them in a peaceful and quiet room, because even background music can affect the way you answer the questions. Also, it is best to have a pen and paper ready so you could jot down the words that you can most identify with in terms of their value to you.

First, think about the happiest moment in your personal life. Visualize the moment in detail in your mind, or you can pick up a photo of that experience to help you remember. Now, answer this question, "What are the factors in this moment in your life that are the reason for making you so happy?"

Now, think about an achievement at school or work you are most proud of. Visualize it in the same way you did with your happiest moment, then when you are ready, answer this second question, "What are the factors in this moment in your career or academic life that contribute to your feelings of success?"

Next, try to recall a moment in your personal life in which you felt most satisfied, in that you felt at the time that your life is so put together. Now, answer these questions: "What was the thing that you desired then that was fulfilled at the time?" and "why did the satisfaction of that desire give you a sense of fulfillment?" After this, you can do the same for your career or academic life.

After you have answered these questions, take a look at the words you have written as you answered each question.

Then, highlight the words that resonate with values to you (such as ambition, balance, belonging, calm, creativity, compassion, discipline, enjoyment, equality, exploration, faith, family, fun, generosity, happiness, health, independence, intelligence, joy, love, loyalty, order, patriotism, perfection, service, strength, and so on). You can also jot down more words to describe these things you value the most.

Once you have your words, your next step is to rank these values according to their importance to you, starting with the top value. The quickest way to figure that out is by asking yourself, "If I could choose only one value to uphold, which one would it be?" Then, you can take it from there.

Once you have highlighted the values that are closest to your heart, you can then check whether they fit in with the kind of life you have right now as well as your future. Try asking yourself questions such as "Do these values that I currently have made me feel proud of myself?"

"Are these values representative of the things that are important to me, even if they are not so common in this society?" "Can these values contribute to my well-being and those of others?" and so on.

Recognizing and understanding your values is as important as it is challenging because it reveals to you your innermost self. No matter what the results are from this exercise, though, be glad and proud of yourself for taking the steps towards becoming more self-aware.

You can learn so much about yourself, especially your innermost hopes, fears, wishes, and values, by using the power of silence. Hopefully, this will not be the last time that you take a step back and reconnect with your inner self because in the years to come you will continue to transform as a person.

It would be good to know if these changes within you are for the better, not only for yourself but also for the people and things you value in life.

Creating your Quiet Space

Charlotte Eriksson, in a popular quote, said that people need to sit alone in a quiet place sometimes, just "to hear your inner voice", instead of letting it drown in the noise of other people and things.

A quiet space is any place where you can enjoy silence the way you want it, without anyone or anything being able to distract you. It can be somewhere as simple as a corner in your bedroom for short, everyday moments of meditation and peace. Or it can be a special destination that serves as your ultimate getaway for rest and relaxation in times when you really need a high dose of silence.

Whatever the case may be, your quiet space serves as your sanctuary where you can listen to your inner self, contemplate on deep questions, and create freely without the influence of outside criticism and judgment.

Not everyone can afford to regularly buy a ticket to an exotic vacation away from the hustle and bustle, of course, so this chapter is dedicated to helping you to find or create your very own quiet space so that you can afford to enjoy to your heart's desire the power of silence.

Designate a "White Space"

The term "white space" originally refers to a blank section of a document that helps keep the texts, illustrations, and other contents organized and separated. Here, white space is a private and quiet spot where you can find solace in solitude and silence, away from the noise in your life.

It is the quintessential place for catharsis as it allows you to talk to yourself aloud, write in your journal, paint, read, meditate, and so on without anyone disturbing you or making you feel self-conscious.

Designating a white space could be easy if you lived alone; your entire apartment or home can serve as your white space. However, it would be a bit more challenging for those who share a place with other people.

If you happen to be in such a situation and you cannot seem to find any white space elsewhere outside your home, one thing you can do is to determine the time of the day when you do have your home to yourself. It is during these times when your place transforms into your white space.

You can make your white space cozy based on how you define comfort and security. Some people like to visually separate their white space from the other parts of their home by hanging up a curtain.

Others like to evoke a meditative atmosphere by hanging tapestries and keeping candles so they could light them each time they enter their white space. Other people like to keep their white space blank such as by keeping an entire corner bare because they find the simplicity of emptiness soothing to their minds.

You could even create a little ritual for your moments of silence if that brings you happiness and comfort. For example, you can put your phone on silent or airplane mode, or better yet put it away, right before you enter your white space.

You can also ease yourself into a more quiet and peaceful mood by doing 5 to 10 minutes of meditation or write a few pages in your journal once you are within your white space.

Silent contemplation can also be had with a hot cup of tea or as you stare at the blank wall. However you wish to keep your white space, what matters is it inspires you to seek silence each time you visit it.

Let Go of Clutter

The thing about noise is it is not limited to sounds alone, for clutter can also have the same effect as noise to your brain. Some people talk about thriving in clutter, but if they know exactly where to find which item regardless of how much stuff they have in a room, then it is not really cluttered, as clutter is defined as a confused jumble of things.

When you look at clutter, your mind is filled with chaos or unwanted thoughts and emotions caused by the sheer disorder.

The idea of having to clean up and organize the clutter seems overwhelming, which is why a lot of people tend to leave the clutter as is, or at least until they "find the time" to deal with them. However, clutter can be dealt with right away, and all the more urgently so if it is starting to cloud your thoughts and affect your mood.

Sorting through the clutter is easy if you approach it in

three steps: Round Up, Sort, and Assign a Spot. This simple process is therapeutic in the sense that you will be compelled to let go of unessential items, and so it also causes you to let go of the baggage that comes with them.

Rounding up means gathering all of the items into one spot so the spot that was once filled with clutter now becomes completely bare, a fresh start. With all the things rounded up, you can then move on to sorting through them.

As you go through each item, consider whether you have used it in the last 3 months. Alternatively, think about whether you would consider buying it again if you came across it. If you do, then assign it a spot in the bare space.

For all the items that you no longer use and would not consider buying, you can gather them into one of two boxes: the donate pile, where the items are still perfectly functioning but no longer serve their purpose in your life; and the recycle pile, or the broken items that could no longer serve their purpose at all.

As soon as you have finished decluttering, you should then immediately drop them off to their designated places so they cannot crawl back into your space.

Once all the clutter has been cleared away from your space, you can go ahead and spend more than a few quiet minutes admiring your work. Enjoy the feeling of happiness one can only get from feeling a sense of ownership towards a beautifully clean and organized space. You could even take this moment express gratitude for the things that you currently own.

After all, not everyone can afford to own the things they want to have. You can also express gratitude for the things that you are letting go, because they have indeed served their purpose at some point in your life. Even the ones that you had impulsively bought and never used served the purpose of making you feel happy the moment you picked them up at the shopping center.

Deep Clean your Space

Aside from removing the unessential items, you can also deep clean your space so it will be refreshed. It is important for your quiet space to be neat and clean space as well, because a clean space contributes to good health of both body and mind.

To deep clean your space, all you need to do is to thoroughly clean everything, even the areas you do not usually touch when you quickly clean your home. The best part about this is you can conduct this simultaneously with decluttering, and the perfect time to do it is right after you have rounded up the items and before you assign a spot for each of the ones you will be choosing.

Since deep cleaning consists of routine tasks, you would be able to use this as a moment to enjoy silence as well. This works especially for those who are not particularly comfortable with staying still for long periods of time as they could not help but keep their hands busy.

Decorate with Peace in Mind

If you want a home office that makes you feel more productive, a kitchen that motivates you to prepare healthy meals, and a bedroom that encourages you to enjoy deep sleep, then the look of your quiet space should be one that evokes peace and quiet.

Each person will certainly have a different take on what can be defined as "peaceful" and "quiet." For some, this would be a minimalist approach, with bare walls and a simple but comfortable cushion on the floor. For others, an empty space looks more cold and isolated than warm and relaxing, so they would prefer a cozy couch with shelves full of books to be the things in their quiet space.

That being said, you should also take into consideration the huge impact of lighting. For instance, some people prefer their windows open, but others like their quiet space to be dark.

Probably you can try borrowing a page from the Danes who value their hygge, which roughly refers to the quality of comfort and coziness, by lighting candles and using lamps with warm bulbs instead of an overhead light whenever you want to use your quiet space.

So, now that you know how to create a quiet space, can you immediately think of a special spot in your home that you can "officially" declare as your own version of what it is? Make this project of transforming that space into one that embraces peace and quiet, because the journey towards creating this special sanctuary is just as therapeutic and relaxing as indulging in the end result itself.

Simplifying your Daily Life

Lin Yutang said that the wisdom of light includes getting rid of the non-essentials. When you simplify your daily life, you make everything in it much easier, quieter, and more balanced, and you can do that by reducing whatever keeps it complicated.

It might seem like such as a big task to have to eliminate things from your life, but in reality, you can actually achieve this in little steps. And besides, the process of simplifying your life should also be simple in and of itself, which can be done by taking things day by day, slowly and mindfully.

You can be as creative and resourceful as you can be when you wish to make your daily life simpler and easier. Just keep in mind, though, that this also means making a few sacrifices.

For example, if you are overworking yourself to earn a lot more money, you might want to reconsider by spending less money instead. That way, you would not have to be too exhausted all the time.

Likewise, you might also have to sacrifice some relationships in your life that are doing you more harm than good, such as with a nosy friend who hogs at least an hour of your time on the phone just for the sake of gossip. It could also mean letting go of things that are cluttering up in your home, even if they have some sort of sentimental value to you.

With all these being said, here are some of the steps you can implement right now to help make your daily routines more quiet and relaxed:

Make Mornings and Evenings Relaxing

You simply cannot control every aspect of your day, but you sure can do something about when and how you spend your time after you wake up and before you go to bed. With this in mind, think about how you can make the start and end of each day more relaxing, peaceful, and motivating for you.

This is especially important to those whose daily lives are filled with so much work and interactions with other people as well as those who live in the city and is always surrounded by movement and noise.

Now, if you are looking for ways to make your mornings simpler so you can usher in the day with a bright, fresh, and positive mindset, one tip to try is to drink water as soon as you wake up.

This will instantly awaken your internal system and at the same time refresh your cells after hours of water deprivation during sleep. You can keep a covered glass of cool water on your bedside table the night before so it will be an effortless habit to keep.

When it comes to rejuvenating your body, you could do yourself a big favor by doing a few simple stretches in bed or right after you get out of it. Stretching wakes up your muscles and boosts your blood flow. Moreover, by doing stretches every morning, you can condition your muscles and joints to be more limber.

Another thing to incorporate into a simple morning routine is to have essentially the same healthy breakfast every day.

For instance, you can have oatmeal every morning for breakfast, and then just add variety on the add-ons, such as pairing it with the fruits of the season and different savory sides such as hard-boiled egg on Mondays, tofu bacon on Tuesdays, and so on. This might sound a bit extreme, but it will really help you out as it eliminates the trouble of having to decide on what to have for breakfast.

As for your night routine, some great habits to incorporate

are to detach yourself from your digital devices at least an hour or two before you go to bed, write out your thoughts in a journal, and practice deep relaxation meditation (entire chapters are dedicated to these tips, so let us not get into detail).

You can also do the things that make you feel more comfortable and relaxed so as to set the mood for sleep. For some, it could be journaling, while for others, it could be writing down a to-do list for the following day. It also helps to take a multivitamin before bed, especially if you are certain that your diet does not really allow you to get your complete required set of vitamins and minerals.

A warm shower or bath one hour before bedtime can also soothe your tired muscles and be quite therapeutic to a stressed out mind. Right after doing so, it would also be ideal to step into a cool, dark, and silent bedroom for it will surely encourage sleep.

However you want to spend your mornings and evenings, the bottom-line is to keep your plan simple enough for you to follow through with it consistently. If there is any aspect of your routine that you feel is cluttering things up, then consider eliminating it or reducing it to a level that is much more comfortable for you.

Streamline your Schedule

Most, if not all, of us, want to do more in less time, but if you want to be efficient and effective without sacrificing your sanity, then what you can do is to take better control over your time each day. This is made easy when you streamline your schedule or, in other words, organize your tasks for the day based on when and for how long you plan to do each.

It is so important to simplify and streamline your schedule because – let's face it – we all have a limited amount of time on our hands. That being said, the first thing to take into consideration before you start mapping out your schedule is the number of hours you have for the day.

For instance, if you need to be in bed by 10 p.m. and awake by 6 a.m. on most days, then that means out of the 24 hours you have, you should deduct 8 hours of sleep. Thus, you are left with 16 hours of waking time which you should then carefully allocate to the right activities.

You can streamline your schedule using a pen and paper or an app on a digital device, but regardless of the medium you choose to use, it is best to do it in a quiet room where not even music can affect your stream of thoughts.

If you are new to this idea, here are some tips on how you can streamline your schedule each day:

Choose a Time of the Day for Scheduling

This might sound overboard, but you really should make an appointment with yourself for scheduling, because by doing so you are making it an unavoidable part of your day. Your schedule will minimize your chances of procrastinating as well as biting off more than you can chew, so scheduling should definitely become a habit.

Some people prefer to plan their day early in the morning, shortly before or after breakfast, because it helps set the right mood for the rest of the day. Others like it better before they go to bed so that when they wake up in the morning they would know exactly what needs to be done.

Once you have decided on the time when you can schedule, you should then determine how long it would take you to plan. Most of the time, it takes 15 to 30 minutes, but you can go with what works for you. You can even use an alarm to remind you to start scheduling, and a timer to prevent you from over-planning.

Recognize your Top Priorities

Before you stuff your day with tasks, think first about the most important task you need to accomplish. Reflect briefly on it is your priority above all the others, and how you would be able to dedicate most of your energy on it for that day. Only after you have set your schedule for that task should you then focus on the remaining ones.

If you have too many tasks in mind, you can write them all down and then make quick adjustments based on your personal needs and preferences. One simple way to do this is to highlight the top three tasks and cross off the unimportant ones. If a task is important but is something you can reschedule to another day or delegate to someone else, then make a note of them.

With this in mind, you would be able to realize the importance of saying "no" to tasks that only add burden to you. Of course, if it is a task that you have agreed upon as a favor to someone and if it is worth the sacrifice of your personal time and energy because this person is important to you, then it should not be considered an irrelevant task.

Focus on One Task at a Time

Multitasking is a fallacy because we are certainly incapable of focusing on more than one task at the same time. Rather, what we do is to switch rapidly from one task to another, and while this might seem efficient at first, it will certainly make you feel more exhausted and it could cause your output to be a lot more "quantity" than "quality."

You can definitely do yourself a big favor by focusing on only one task at a time, and to not stop until you have reached your desired level of progress on the task before you switch to another one.

Time blocking is a great scheduling strategy to apply if your goal is to ensure that you will practice the habit of single-tasking. To do this, all you need to do is to assign a specific period of time for a specific task, or a specific day for a particular project.

For example, if your goal is to have a fixed morning routine, then you can time block 6 to 7 a.m. for your early morning exercise and a quick shower.

Then, you can time block 7:30 a.m. to 9 a.m. for breakfast, getting ready for work, and commuting to the office. After that, you can time block your 9 to 5 specifically for appointments at work, before you time block 5 to 6 p.m. for the commute back to your home, and so on.

The great thing about streamlining your schedule is it will simplify your day. At the same time, it will enable you to see an overview of exactly when you have free time and for how long. Moreover, it will sharpen your focus on the task that has been time blocked because that particular time-frame is the only period you have for it.

All in all, the quickest way to simplify your day is to identify and get rid of anything that does not serve a meaningful purpose to your life. That way, you can eliminate bad habits such as spending too much time on social media, idle chatter and overworking on projects where you are underpaid.

At the same time, you can dedicate more of your time and energy of the day on exercise, cooking healthy meals at home, and enjoying quality periods of quiet and rest.

4 - Unplugging from the Digital Noise

"We get sucked into the Internet and streaming information, and it's time to just unplug and look within."

Jonathan Cain

Nowadays, much of the noise most of us experience actually comes from our digital devices. More specifically, they come from all of the input we could get from whatever it is we had downloaded into our phones or computers – games, e-books, and so on – or the internet. Take a look at your social media feed, for instance, because you can clearly see how bombarded it is with information.

Yet, most of what you see is not actually relevant to you or is something you care for.

Be that as it may, because we so yearn to find something – anything – that we might just find to be interesting or useful to us, we continue to scroll down and down until we perhaps encounter something that is someone funny or thought-provoking or concerning, that we would feel a sense of accomplishment for having come across it.

Little do most of us know, all of these texts, pictures, videos, sounds, and other sensory input contribute to information overload or overexposure to data or information.

Information overload has a lot of negative effects, and according to sociologist Georg Simmel, it could cause people to become exhausted too easily, to the point where they could no longer respond effectively to new situations. Moreover, being overexposed to data leads to poor decision-making because, let's face it, most of us can only process a limited amount of information at a time.

On the other hand, writer, teacher, and consultant Clay Shirky states that we do not suffer from information overload; rather, he calls it "filter failure."

In other words, we cannot really blame the fact that all the information is within reach now, thanks to our digital devices, but what we can do to solve the problem of information overload is to control what kind of information we allow ourselves to access when we should access them, and how.

That said, we should designate a certain time of the day to remove ourselves from the vortex of information overload via a digital detox.

A "digital detox" is a specific time-frame in which you do not make use of any electronic devices – be it your phone, your computer, the television, and so on – for the primary purpose of reducing stress, lowering anxiety, and enhancing your appreciation of the physical world. A digital detox is a perfect time to enjoy the power of silence as well.

Multiple studies can support the notion that doing this regularly can increase your mental health, boost your emotional intelligence, enhance your relationships with the people around you, increase your productivity, and even improve your body posture.

Of course, it is up to you on when and for how long you should do it, but if you are looking for some guidelines and tips, here are some great ways on how to make the most out of your digital detox:

Highlight the Why

Do you think going on a digital detox is important to you? If you do, then ask yourself what your reasons behind it are.

Some people do it because they want to enhance their creativity and productivity, and mindless noise on the television or the internet is keeping them from hearing themselves think.

Others want to go on a digital detox because seeing all the updates from their friends on social media is causing them to become more and more envious, and this sense of self-awareness is telling them to take charge before it gets any worse.

There are also those who wish to enjoy the time they could spend with the people who are actually right next beside them, but their digital devices are keeping them from being in the present moment.

Find out what your motivations are for wanting to go on a digital detox because these will help you stick to your schedule no matter how tempting it is to stay hooked.

Identify your Digital Detox Time

Some people can afford to just spontaneously decide to go on a digital detox for 24 to 48 hours, but for others, this can be unrealistic, especially if their work requires them to go online every now and then. Whatever your case may be, it would be best to choose a specific time-frame for you to go on a digital detox.

For instance, if you know for a fact that you do not really need to go online and check your work email after 5 pm, then your digital detox can start there. You can also treat your days off as digital detox times.

The first hour of your day, or right from the moment you wake up, is a good time to go on a digital detox. Let this be a quiet moment with nothing but you and your thoughts as you prepare your breakfast, shower, and do all of the other things that need to be done to start your day right.

At least an hour before your bedtime is also a good time to start a digital detox because this will not only give you the peace and quiet you so need to be in the mood for sleep but also prevent you from developing insomnia. This is because the blue light emitted from a digital screen tricks the brain into thinking it is still daytime, thus preventing you from transitioning to sleep mode.

An alternative way to do a digital detox is to set a daily limit for the time you spend on your devices, instead of scheduling a period for your detox. This strategy is especially helpful to some people because it makes them become more selective of the kind of information they choose online as well as how they interact with their devices.

This is also effective for those whose work actually requires them to use digital devices, such as online writers and computer programmers because their limit will cause them to focus much of their "plugged in" time on work.

Keep in mind that you can always reschedule your digital detox depending on your needs and preferences. What matters is you stick to it regularly.

Develop Digital Detox Habits

Aside from setting a schedule, another way to reduce the amount of time you spend on your digital devices is to develop specific habits that will eventually make it effortless for you to do so. To help you get started, here are some common digital detox habits that you can apply to your life right now:

No Phones during Mealtimes

Put away your smartphone during mealtimes, regardless of whether you are eating alone or with family. You can even talk to your family and friends about this and practice "phone stacking," or putting all of your devices in a box or in the middle of the table before the meal.

You can even come up with rules to help impose this habit, such as by footing the bill or buying desserts for everyone if you are the first person to pick your phone up before meal-time is over.

No Text, No Call while Driving

Keep is to put your phone on silent mode and store it away while you are driving. This will save not just your life one day, but others on the road, too. Understand that no phone call could be so important that you would risk it all just to answer it.

"Screen Free" Bed

A really good habit to keep is to make your bed a "screen free" zone, in that you will not ever bring your phone or your laptop, or any other digital device to it. Give it a try and you will notice that you will sleep much better later on. Besides, if you are using your phone as an alarm clock you will be more likely to get out of bed if it is not within reach as soon as it wakes you up.

From these habits, you can also start coming up with your own to reduce the amount of time you spend each day in front of a screen.

Make your Digital Detox Enjoyable

There are so many great activities you could engage in while on a digital detox, the most invigorating of which is to commune with nature. Since an entire chapter in this book is dedicated to that, it will not be discussed in detail here. Aside from it, here are some of the ways in which you can enjoy your digital detox:

Enjoy an "at home" spa

Indulging in some "me" time during a digital detox does not have to cost a lot of money. In fact, more people have been recreating the spa-like treatment within the comforts of their own home.

One way you can do that is to dim the lights, light some scented candles, run a warm bath, pop into it a bath bomb, and then soak yourself for a few minutes in its rejuvenating waters. As you do, you can take your time exfoliating your skin, deep conditioning your hair, and all of the other "spa" things people do. You can also pour yourself a glass of wine and just enjoy this still and quiet moment.

Re-visit your favorite books

Sometimes, we get so caught up with the happenings in the digital arena that we forget the nostalgic charm we used to enjoy when we read paperbacks. But if we take the time to put down our phones and open those old books again, we could transport ourselves back to the old, familiar world that once enraptured us.

The beautiful thing about re-reading your old favorites from so many years ago is that you would be able to interpret the messages and stories in them now that your mindset and perspectives in life have changed. So, go ahead and cuddle up with your favorite book and the drink you used to enjoy while reading it in a quiet and cool corner, even just for an hour or two.

Try doodling or sketching

Making art is a cheap and easy way to relax, let your creative juices flow, and enjoy peace and quiet. You can express yourself in any way you wish through your sketches, paintings, colors, pencils, and all your other art media in a quiet library or peaceful park.

One benefit to putting away your digital devices and turning to more traditional forms of art is it helps enhance your focus and reduce your stress levels at the same time. Your work can also represent the thoughts and feelings coming from deep within your inner self.

Some would even scribble for a few minutes with their eyes closed because this helps them loosen up as well as get to know another side of themselves. If you want to give this a try, here is how you can do it:

Get a piece of paper and tape its edges against a table. Grab a box of crayons and place it somewhere that makes it easy for you to reach them. When you are ready, take a few deep breaths to relax before you grab a crayon. Then, close your eyes and allow your hands to just scribble to your heart's desire. After you are done with your "eyes closed" scribble, you can go ahead and examine your output.

Aside from these simple but relaxing activities that you can do without a digital device, there are plenty of other suggestions to explore throughout this book. But as you can see, going on a digital detox is something everyone can look forward to each day. Enjoy silence just as much as you enjoy your digital detox, and your mind and heart will be truly filled.

5 - Introspecting through Journaling

"In the journal, I do not just express myself more openly than I could to any person; I create myself."

Susan Sontag

Everyone experiences ups and downs in life, regardless of whether they would define theirs as simple or complex. There are happy times just as there are sad, moments of anger just as there are of love and plenty of other emotions and experiences in between.

All these cannot be avoided, but sometimes it is important to take a step back from these so as to not feel overwhelmed. It is during these moments of "stepping back" that we are able to keep ourselves from being consumed by the noise of life.

It is a quiet time when we can reconnect with our true passions and goals and truly get to know our inner selves. And in these moments, we can appreciate the power of silence.

One of the most effective ways to release all of your emotions and clarify most if not all of your thoughts, in true silence that is free from distraction, is through journaling. To keep a journal means to write regularly in a notebook everything that crosses your mind. Susan Sontag said that you are creating your own self when you write a journal, more than expressing yourself.

Most of the time, people record their daily experiences in a journal, while others stick to a certain "theme" by writing only poems or songs, or doodling, or retelling only the highlights of their life in their journal.

If you have not started journaling yet, or if you used to and had forgotten how good it was for you, then it helps to know that it is really good for your mental and emotional well-being.

For instance, regular writing helps spark creativity as well as enhances your concentration. Writing out your thoughts and emotions is therapeutic as well, in the sense that it enables you to "transfer" them from your mind to paper.

The best part about journaling is there are no judgments. You are free to write whatever is on your mind. There is no standard set of criteria to determine whether you are doing a good job of journaling or not. In a way, it is a lot like meditation, because what matters is you are doing it.

Of course, you are more likely to write your thoughts smoothly the more frequently you write, but it is okay if you still struggle to put into words how you feel no matter how many entries you have made.

That being said, you might still be looking for ideas on how you can start keeping a journal. Here are some guidelines that you can turn to, but again, you are free to approach your experience in journaling in any way you prefer.

Paper, Digital, or Online

Back then, people were only able to journal on paper, but now you can choose whether to write in a paper notebook, in a device, or via a blog.

When it comes to journaling on paper, there is something romantic about writing in a secret notebook that you can hide away in your sock drawer, and there is something comforting about seeing your thoughts being translated into written words in your own handwriting.

Using the digital medium for journaling can also have its benefits. For one, you can keep thousands of entries in a single device instead of having to buy paper notebooks each time.

You can also easily search for a previous entry just by typing in some keywords and then letting the device pull them up for you, in case you want to go back on a quote you wrote or a memory you had recorded from long ago. The biggest setback with a digital diary, though, is if something happens to your device. In such cases, all your entries would get wiped out.

If you are not fond of writing on paper and you are worried about losing your device, then what you can do is journal online. Some people like to keep a secret blog in which they remain anonymous as they post all of their thoughts and emotions online.

Others like to keep their entries in a password encrypted drive, which means they can access their journal anywhere and would not have to worry about losing their entries in case their device crashes. The only thing they could worry about is if they get hacked.

No matter what type of medium you choose for journaling, the bottom-line is it can help you to enjoy being in the midst of silence as you release your thoughts and emotions from your mind to it. Journaling should always be a source of comfort and joy for anyone, after all.

Try Journaling Prompts

Currently, there are plenty of special journaling products that contain "prompts" – questions or quotes that inspire you to start writing. You can start with those if you always find yourself at a loss for words whenever you try to start an entry. You can also try answering any one of the following journaling prompts below each time you wish to write something:

Prompts for Discovering your Inner Self

What is the one memory in your mind that brings so much nostalgia to your heart? Describe the memory by engaging all your senses: what you see, hear, smell, feel, and even taste.

- Write a letter to your future self (your 20 years older self, perhaps?). Describe what life is like right now, especially what you are currently into, who are the people you spend most of your time with, and so on.

- Write a letter to your past self (yourself 10 years ago, maybe?). Talk about how far you have gone now and how much you have accomplished so far your passions, and the important people in your life.

- Confess the worst thing you have ever done, and how you feel about it. Write about what you can do to forgive yourself for this transgression.

- Write about your biggest but most secret desire. Why do you want it so much and is it possible for you to acquire it?

- Write about the craziest thing you have ever done in your whole life. Describe it in detail and explain why you think it is crazy.

- What is on your mind right now? Write down what you think of it, how you feel about it, and what you can do about it.

Prompts to Boost Productivity

- What is your biggest achievement in life and how were you able to do it? Why do you think this moment in your life made you feel successful?

- Describe your biggest life goal in vivid detail. Explain your reason for having this goal, then write down what you need to achieve first before you can acquire it, how much time you think it will take you to achieve it, and so on.

- When do you feel most productive? Why do you think it is that particular time? What have you been able to achieve during those times?

- What do you think you need to do in order to move closer towards achieving your goal?

- What are your top five biggest strengths that can help you achieve your goal? How would you be able to wield each of them to do this?

- Think of someone successful that you have always looked up to. What qualities do they have that make them so admirable? What were the struggles they had to go through before they achieved success in life?

- When was the last time you got distracted? What could be the reason behind it? What can you do to avoid this distraction in the future?

Prompts for Relaxation and Peace of Mind

- What has been causing you an unusual level of stress lately? Write each of them down, and then explain why they are your source of stress and what you can do reduce them in your life.

- Make a list of all the people and things that make you feel happy. Express gratitude for each of these. Choose from the list the ones that are closest to your heart and describe in detail your fondest memory of them.

- "If you want to forget something or someone, never hate it, or never hate him/her. Everything and everyone that you hate is engraved upon your heart; if you want to let go of something, if you want to forget, you cannot hate." What do you make of this quote by C. Joybell C.?

- When was the last time you truly felt rested and relaxed? Do you think you need more of these? How would you be able to get enough of it?

- Think about a specific area near you that immediately evokes peace and relaxation the moment you think of it (you could even print out a picture of it and paste it in your journal). Why qualities of this place make it so? When would you be able to visit this place?

- Write about how you would like to spend a day free from responsibilities. Where would you like to go? Who will you spend time with? What will you do? How will you feel by the end of that day?

Prompts for Enhancing your Relationships with Others

- Create a list of all the people in your life who love, support, and accept you wholeheartedly. You could even draw their faces or post a picture of them next to their names. Then, write down your most fond memory with them. If that person is still around think about how you could spend more time with them.

- Write a letter to each of the most important people in your life. If you want to forgive or if you want to be forgiven by that person, how much you appreciate them, miss them, love them, or simply enjoy their everyday company. Let it be as heartfelt as you wish. Sending those letters out is optional, but if you feel that they could enhance your relationship with these people, then, by all means, do so.

- Challenge yourself to come up with a list of 50 ways you could express love and kindness to others, whether they are humans or animals. Then, challenge yourself to try to do one thing on the list every day.

- If you could do one thing for someone else, throw them a surprise party, take them to a nice vacation spot, buy them something they have always wanted, or whatever you think is best for that person, who would it be and what would you do? Plan it in detail. Then, if you wish, you could go ahead and do just that.

- Hopefully, this chapter has inspired you to get into the habit of journaling, even for just 5 minutes per day. The early morning would be a great time to do so because your surroundings would still be peacefully cool and quiet. Writing things down before turning in for the night can also increases your chances of a good night's sleep. Come to think of it, you can journal anytime you wish, for in silence you would not only be able to hear yourself think but write about it, too.

Meditating in Silence

Meditation, in general, is defined as the practice of contemplating deeply and continuously on a particular subject. A growing number of people are practicing meditation, mostly because of the praise it got from famous and successful people, including Steve Jobs, Oprah Winfrey, Richard Gere, and Hugh Jackman, to name a few. Even the big companies have started encouraging their employees to meditate.

Jobs, for instance, allowed his employees at Apple to practice half an hour of meditation during working hours every day and would even sponsor meditation sessions at the office.

One of Google's perks is offering their employees meditation courses because they believe it will improve their mental health as well as their performance at work. Nike also encourages meditation in the workplace and even has relaxation rooms where their employees can practice meditation.

As for the different ways to meditate, there certainly are plenty. However, in this particular case, we will be putting much emphasis on a simple yet highly beneficial and relevant type of meditation, which is to meditate in silence.

The paradox of silent meditation is that the longer you practice it, the more it uncovers a different kind of noise – your innermost thoughts. As a result, you will find that the noise surrounding you each day does not compare to the noise that could be buried deep inside your mind. Be that as it may, it is good to be fully aware of these thoughts and to accept them, for only then would you be able to let them go.

Another paradox of silent meditation is it is not meant to silence the mind. Rather, you are to listen to your mind as it brings to the surface more deep-seated thoughts, feelings, memories, and expectations. By allowing yourself only silence in the outside world, your mind will finally be able to feel honest towards itself.

If you want to give silent meditation a try, here are some great techniques to start with.

6 - Deep Breathing Meditation

Have you ever stopped to appreciate how your body continues to keep you alive by breathing?

This is but one of the questions that arise to mind in most of those who have developed an appreciation for breathing meditation. More importantly, this technique has helped many people lower their anxiety, improve focus, and encourage deep thought.

Breathing meditation can be practiced anywhere, but you will find that it is most effective when done in a quiet and peaceful room. So, give it a try right now by keeping in mind the following steps:

Step 1: Find a quiet space, preferably with fresh air, where no one will disturb you.

A shady area at the park is a great place to do deep breathing meditation, but essentially you can do it anywhere as long as the air is clean and fresh. Once you are in that place, you can sit or lie down comfortably, but make sure to keep your back straight and your shoulders relaxed.

Step 2: Place one hand on your abdomen and the other on your chest.

Doing this will enhance your deep breathing technique because the key is that your abdomen – not your chest – should be the one rising and falling as you take in your deep breaths. By putting one hand on each spot, you can easily determine that.

Step 3: Take a few deep breaths before starting.

While there are no techniques set in stone when it comes to deep breathing, most people still want to have some sort of guideline on how long they should inhale, hold their breath, and exhale.

If you happen to be one of them, then you can try inhaling slowly through your nostrils for 4 seconds until your lungs are completely filled. Then, hold it in for 2 seconds before you slowly exhale through your mouth for a slow 8 seconds.

Practice this technique a few times, and when you are ready, you can proceed to enter the meditative state.

Step 4: Relax your eyelids and concentrate on your breath.

It helps to gently think, I am about to do deep breathing meditation so that you can set the right mood for the session. Begin with your natural breath, then slowly inhale, allowing your mind to focus on the movement of the air as it fills your lungs.

As you hold your breath, concentrate on how your muscles respond to the expansion of your lungs. Notice, in particular, the area around your throat, shoulders, upper back, and chest. It should not be painful.

As you exhale, trace the breath as it leaves your body and dissipates into the air. Give yourself a second or two to relax before you move on to the next inhale.

Step 5: Relax your body with each deep breath.

As you continue to breathe deeply, notice if there is any tension in any part of your body. Once you spot one, imagine each breath being concentrated in that area. Continue to "breathe into" that spot until it starts to relax. You can also visualize the tension leaving your body as you exhale.

Step 6: Relax your mind with each deep breath.

After your body is completely relaxed, gently shift your focus towards your mind. Observe your mind as if you are a person looking in, and notice if there is any tension or disturbance in it.

If you do notice a disturbing thought, a painful feeling, or anything that strains your mind, breathe deeply and visualize these thoughts exiting your body with each exhale. Continue to do so until your mind feels completely light and at peace.

When you are ready to come out of deep breathing meditation, do not make the end abrupt. Instead, draw yourself out of it by gently reverting back to your natural breath. Give yourself a few minutes to relax in natural breathing as well before you stand up and go about your day.

7 - Five Minutes of Silent Meditation

This simple technique can be practiced by any beginner to meditation, but what makes it so thought-provoking is how it can actually give you a fresh perspective on time. The only way to understand it is to practice it yourself, but before you begin make sure to have a clock or your watch close by. Now, here are the steps:

Step 1: Settle in your quiet space.

You may sit down on a chair or on a cushion on the floor. Keep a straight back but maintain relaxed shoulders. You can shift around until you find a position that is comfortable for you.

Step 2: Ease yourself into the meditative state.

Before the start of the meditation, check the time. As soon as a new minute starts, close your eyes and quietly think, "I am about to meditate for five minutes." Then, focus on your natural breath.

Step 3: Allow yourself to be open and curious.

As you continue to focus on your breath, notice how your mind reacts. It might start to think about how long it has been since you started, when the three minutes is up, and so on. Whatever thoughts cross your mind, let them fade away until you can draw yourself back to the sensation of your natural breath.

Step 4: Gently ease yourself out of the meditative state once you think the five minutes are up.

Continue to focus on your breath until you cannot help but think that it has indeed been five minutes. Once you feel that the time is up, you can gently open your eyes and check the clock or watch.

Step 5: Determine whether you were able to end the meditation at the right time.

As soon as you have opened your eyes, check to see if you really were able to meditate for exactly five minutes based solely on your intuition.

However, it does not really matter whether you stopped at exactly minutes or not because what really matters is how it allows you to really stop and reflect on your perspective of time. With more practice, you will be able to sharpen your intuition on time as well as develop an appreciation of the present moment and the fleeting of time itself.

You can start practicing silent meditation during your quiet time and in your quiet space, but eventually, you will learn to practice it anywhere and at any time of the day. For instance, you can spend even just 5 minutes of your 15-minute break at work on it, or you can practice it before you go to bed at night.

Regardless of the length of your meditation, though, what matters is you do it regularly. That way, your mind will always have its moment of clarity no matter how noisy or busy your life can get.

8 - Connecting with Nature

Silence in the midst of nature has got to be the most beautiful way to relax and get away from the noise of life, even for just a little while. In fact, it has been scientifically proven that nature can heal the mind and body in many ways. Rachel Carson couldn't have said it any better than those who stop to appreciate the beauty of the earth, become more energized and they find the strength that lasts a lifetime.

For instance, getting a healthy dose of sunlight outdoors will grant you your much-needed vitamin D, which helps strengthen your bones and teeth by improving your body's ability to absorb calcium. Moreover, vitamin D is a natural mood booster as it reduces blood pressure and enhances blood flow.

Aside from the sunshine, you can also inhale as much fresh air as you want in nature. This is in stark contrast to the polluted and stuffy air you would usually get in the city, which causes the lungs to work twice as hard just to get the oxygen from it.

It is also good to know that serotonin or the neurotransmitter that is responsible for your memory, mood, and social behavior is directly linked to the amount of oxygen in your body. If your serotonin levels are low, you will feel sluggish and even depressed.

But since nature's fresh air makes it almost effortless for your lungs to get the oxygen it needs, your serotonin levels will become regulated and you will feel much more relaxed and happy. With this in mind, it would be a good idea for you to practice deep breathing while you are in nature so you can make the most of the clean air.

Being in nature also helps reduce the stress you would naturally get from the demands of your daily routine. You can maximize this by engaging in some fun activities while in nature to also increase the level of endorphins in your system. Endorphin is another neurochemical that can boost your mood when the brain is triggered to produce it.

Now, some may already agree with all of these, but if you are the type of person who is so used to the urban landscape, then now is the time to give the great outdoors a try. To give you some ideas, here are some ways on how you can immerse in the power of silence by connecting with nature:

Go trail running or riding

Trail running, also called fell or mountain running is the name of a sport wherein you would run and hike over trails. Trail riding is also done in the same terrain, except you are crossing the trail on a mountain bike instead of on foot. Most places have a safe and controlled nature park where people can follow a trail for the purpose of exercise.

If you want to know the trails in your area, you can ask your local running or biking clubs and stores as well as national park offices. You can also ask your friends on social media because at least one of them might just be a running enthusiast.

Trail running and riding are great ways to get a lot of oxygen into your system while enjoying the natural scenery. Just make sure that the trail you have chosen for this activity is secure before you start. Also, if you are new to the area it would be advisable for you to invite some friends to come with you or to bring your dog and for you to go there in the early morning rather than the evening.

To make your trail running experience truly enjoyable, wear shoes that are built for the trail, because you will be encountering some mud, puddles, roots, rocks, and other such materials across the terrain and regular running shoes might not be able to handle them. Always bring some water with you and put on sunscreen before you go out as well as some bug repellant.

Swim in the lake or at the beach

If you are fortunate enough to be living close to a beach or lake, then you should certainly make the most of it. Swimming leisurely in a natural pool of water, that is guaranteed safe, of course, is another great way to enjoy peace and quiet in the midst of nature.

The beach, for instance, is the quintessential picture of relaxation. Enjoy the natural sound of the waves crashing against the shore or, better yet, swim in deep if you know how and enjoy the peaceful stillness below.

You could even wear a pair of goggles so you can enjoy watching the world of corals, fishes, and sea plants underneath. Just take care not to go swimming without a life guard unless you are a certified professional.

Try Cloud Gazing or Bird Watching

Wherever you may be, you can certainly enjoy such simple outdoor activities as cloud gazing and bird watching. All you ever really need is a nearby plain where you can spread out a nice blanket, lie down, and look up at the skies.

You could even bring a little picnic basket of goodies with you to make the experience more fun. This might sound a bit cheesy, but the opportunity to take pleasure in such activities is being taken for granted by most of us who are so hooked to our computers.

If you want to give cloud gazing a try, you would be glad to know that there is actually a meditation practice called Sky Gazing, because it uses the sky as a metaphor of one's state of mind while practicing it.

You can even liken the noise in your life – your worries, anxieties, and bad memories – to clouds and your mind as the sky, in that they do cross the sky but they never really stay there. Be on the lookout for clouds that embody certain thoughts that cross your mind, and then watch them float away and take those troublesome thoughts along with them.

As for bird-watching, all you really need is a good pair of

binoculars, some quality time for solitude, and a regional field guide to help you identify the local birds. The wonderful thing about this activity is you will learn to appreciate different species of birds and really become more in tune with life in nature.

Give it a try once or twice, with a borrowed pair of binoculars, at the park or in any nature spot where you are likely to find different kinds of birds. For starters, you will be able to find songbirds within the first two hours after the sun rises and before the sun sets. If you are a big fan of eagles and hawks, in particular, then you should be on the lookout for them before the crack of dawn.

Remember to be very quiet because you might scare them away. If you find yourself being more drawn to this activity, you could even join a birding group so you can all silently enjoy the experience of bird watching together.

You do not have to spend a lot of money to enjoy nature of course, although there is definitely nothing wrong with going on a great nature getaway. It is just as pleasurable to enjoy a sunny picnic, meditate, or read a good book underneath a shady tree at the park, or hop on a bus to a nearby beach.

Find the time to connect with nature and enjoy the silence there, for only then would you be able to appreciate that the world – and all its wonder – is much bigger than all of your problems combined.

9 - Rekindling the Joy of Reading

"To acquire the habit of reading is to construct for yourself a refuge from almost all the miseries of life."

W. Somerset Maugham

Most adults, even those who would describe themselves to be readers when they were younger, now struggle to find the time to fully immerse themselves in a good book. Sometimes, they would buy a book and "read" it because they feel that they should, or because it is a popular piece with an upcoming movie adaptation.

However, all too often people end up not finishing the books they have started to read or, worse, only skim through the book instead of allowing it to transport them to the universe contained within its pages as it should.

If you have lost your genuine love for reading or if you have never been a reader, then it is time to use the power of silence to rekindle your joy of it. Here are the best strategies you can apply right now to find true pleasure in reading without getting distracted by the noise of the outside world:

Dedicate a Special Quiet Place and Time for Reading

If you think you do not have enough time for pleasurable reading, then the solution is to make time for it. Set an appointment with yourself just to enjoy a good story, whether it is on the weekend or an hour before bedtime, and then stick to it.

Let your quiet space be your little reading nook as well so that each time you enter it you would be motivated to pick up where you left off in the story. Former bookworms also find that they are more drawn back to the world of books each time they enter an old library, so if you want you can also become a member of one and then spend your quiet time there, just for reading.

Start with Short Fiction

Truth be told, not everyone has the luxury of time to read an entire novel, for all avid readers, know that the best way to read a good novel is to not stop until it is finished. If you happen to be someone who could spare only a short amount of time and energy on reading, then your next best adventure to take aside from a novel would be in the form of short stories.

Short stories typically have less than 8,000 words, which means that an average person can finish reading it within 45 minutes. The best part is that there are thousands of free short stories online, and all you have to do is browse through the list of titles based on your favorite genre.

If you are looking for some ideas, here is a list of some of the most profound classic and modern short fiction stories and books to try:

- The Most Dangerous Game by Richard Connell (1924)

- The Lottery by Shirley Jackson (1948)

- A Good Man is Hard to Find by Flannery O'Connor (1953)

- A Sound of Thunder by Ray Bradbury (1952)

- The Tell-Tale Heart by Edgar Allan Poe (1843)

- A Very Short Story by Ernest Hemingway (1924)

- The Celebrated Jumping Frog of Calaveras County by Mark Twain (1865)

- Interpreter of Maladies by Jhumpa Lahiri (1999)

- Seven Lives to Repay Our Country by Edward H. Carpenter (2011)

- Home by Alice Munro (2006)

- In Hindsight by Callan Wink (2015)

- What Happened to the Baby? By Cynthia Ozick (2006)

Stop and Move On

This might sound sacrilegious to hardcore readers out there, but if you are reading a story, book, or article that you simply do not find interesting, then, by all means, stop reading it and move on to another one. Even the best authors cannot please everyone, so no matter how much others have been raving about a particular book. Drop it if you yourself cannot find pleasure in its characters, theme, and plot.

That being said, it is also a good idea to try to explore beyond your comfort zone of genres every now and then. For instance, if all you have been reading since childhood is sci-fi, then maybe you could also try historical fiction.

If you are fond of adventure, you might also discover that you actually find satire enjoyable. Just continue to explore more pieces until you find ones that really make you want to read more deeply each day.

Go Back to Paper Books

While digital books can save you storage space and money, it simply cannot beat the old world charm of reading paper books. Of course, this does not mean you should cut out e-books entirely. Rather, it would help your mind and eyes to read paper books every now and then.

One idea to help you find joy in reading again is to buy the latest novel or novella of your favorite author. That way, you know for a fact that you enjoy that author's writing style and the time and money you spend on the paper book is worth the investment.

If you have read all of your favorite author's books and he or she has not published anything lately, or if you have never been fond of reading but would like to start, then you can try the "tested and proven" ones.

In other words, pick up the popular books that are always on the New York Times bestseller list based on the genre that you prefer the most. The good thing about doing this is you will not have to worry about not finding a copy at your local bookstore. In fact, they would most likely be on display themselves.

Reach for Graphic Novels

One "hack" to help you start reading again is to find and enjoy a really well-done graphic novel. Graphic novels are basically books consisting of long fictional work, but instead of the story being told in written form, it is mostly in drawn or comic-strip form, with only the dialogue and bits of narrative in the text.

Graphic novels are great for those who are still easing themselves into the world of reading but are still a bit intimidated by the long sentences and complexity of written stories.

If you are looking for some suggestions, here are some of the best graphic novels to date:

- Batman: The Dark Knight Returns by Frank Miller (1986)

- Watchmen (Titan Edition) (1986)

- The Sandman: Dream country by Neil Gaiman (1991)

- Ant Colony by Michael DeForge (2014)

- Teratoid Heights by Mat Brinkman (2000)

- A Drunken Dream and Other Stories by Moto Hagio (2010)

- Baby Bjornstrand by Renée French (2014)

- The Furry Trap by Josh Simmons (2012)

- Meat Cake Bible by Dame Darcy (2016)

Clearly, there are plenty of paths to take if you want to build the habit of reading for pleasure. And this becomes so much easier the moment you find peace in solitude and silence.

10 - Conclusion

Now that you have reached the end of this book, it is safe to assume that you have developed a deep appreciation for silence and solitude and that you are about to apply some of the things you have just learned into your life if you have not already.

Each time you start to feel overwhelmed by the noise of life, always remember to go back to the pages of this book to remind yourself that you can step away from it all, even just for a bit, through the power of silence.

Try not to be too hard on yourself by spending some quiet time to think and breathe deeply in your quiet space, let out your hopes and fears on paper, enjoy the scent of fresh air and the beauty of nature, and introspect so you can reconnect with your inner self. By spending even just a few minutes in peaceful silence, you can positively impact the rest of your day.

Book 3 - Mindset Mastery

Take Back Your Life And Overcome Limitations (Destroy Negative Energy, Be More Confident, Build Smart Habits)

1 - Introduction

Do you often find yourself procrastinating and feeling uninspired?

Do you need help overcoming negative energy?

Are you looking for ways to becoming more confident and motivated?

If your answers to these questions is a resounding "yes!" then this book is definitely for you.

This book is all about helping you discover ways in which you can gain the energy and confidence to unleash your true potential.

You will learn how to develop a winning mindset, enhance Emotional Intelligence, become self-motivated, develop confidence in yourself, take better care of your body, be more productive, build smart habits, and so much more!

With each chapter, you will understand the benefits you will gain for each skill you will learn. More importantly, you will be able to take immediate action simply by following the how-to guides provided afterward. In short, this book aims to not only inspire you, but also to let you take action and become the master of your mindset.

1 - INTRODUCTION

This book is dedicated to you and everyone else who wants to make the most out of their life by starting with their mindset. It is written especially for those who are looking to take back their life, destroy negative energy, and enjoy a happier, healthier, and much more successful self.

Time waits for no one, so begin your journey towards a strong and positive mindset right away. Go ahead and turn to Chapter 1 to start!

2 - Understanding How Your Mindset Works

Have you ever been in a conversation with yourself in your head?

Some people might call it crazy, but the truth is that they themselves are also doing it from time to time. It is what psychologists call "inner speech," and it is described as a silent expression of your own conscious and logical flow of thoughts.

When you are trying to convince yourself not to eat a second (or third) slice of cake, or trying to talk yourself into working out in the early morning, you are engaging in inner speech.

While inner speech is something that happens in all of us on a daily basis, we do not all share the same types of thoughts. In fact, one of the biggest factors that influence our inner speech is our Emotional Intelligence. This is our capability to become aware of our own emotions, as well as those of others.

It also includes our ability to recognize the range of emotional information in order to not just suitably name them, but also to be able to think, behave, and adjust and adapt ourselves appropriately based on them. In this sense, our level of Emotional Intelligence directs the manner in which we engage in inner speech.

At this point, you might be wondering how all of this relates to your mindset. Well, considering inner speech is largely directed by your Emotional Intelligence, it is now time to think about how you usually engage in a conversation with yourself. In other words, how would you describe the way in which you usually engage in a conversation with yourself?

Whatever the nature of your inner speech is, the important thing to consider is that it gives you a peek into how your mindset works. Take note that your mindset is described as your habitual mental attitude that directs you towards interpreting and responding to all given circumstances in your life.

For example, if you noticed that your inner speech almost always consists of negative talk ("you are not good enough," "you are such a failure," "why can't I be more attractive and popular?"), then it gives you an idea that you are feeding a pessimistic mindset.

On the other hand, if a person's inner speech is just a little bit too condescending ("I am better than everyone else in this room," "they are not from an important university, unlike me," or "I'm so glad I am not as ugly as she is") then it is possible for him or her to have an egotistical mindset.

All of these lead you back to one strong source – Emotional Intelligence.

Yes, there are other equally important factors, such as economic (or to be more specific, financial, because your financial stability to some extent does play a role on your inner speech), social and cultural (because the society in which you live largely influences your thoughts and values), and environmental (your physical surroundings and the people in it have a much stronger impact on one's mindset that what most people give them credit for).

However, these factors we have little to no control over. What we can immediately do something about is our inner speech, specifically through our Emotional Intelligence.

This leads us to the big question: "How do we understand how our mindset works?" You can discover the answer to this yourself after you read the next two sections:

3 - Getting to Know the Fixed versus Growth Mindset

We all experience unique situations in our everyday lives, but when it comes to our range of emotions, we share a lot of commonalities. That is to say, we all experience a variety of levels of the same emotions: sadness, happiness, anger, and so on.

That being said, how we feel towards a given situation may vary according to the kind of mindset we have nurtured through the years. This kind may fall between one of the two recognized classifications of mindset, which are the Fixed Mindset and the Growth Mindset. This concept was first established by Dr. Carol Dweck, a psychology professor and researcher who focused on the field of motivation.

A "Fixed Mindset," according to Dweck, is when a learner believes that his or her basic intelligence, abilities, and talents are "fixed traits." Specifically, those with a fixed mindset believe that all they have is a "fixed" amount of positive qualities, and therefore they strive "to look smart all the time," and at the same time, work hard to avoid looking "dumb."

On the other hand, Dweck describes a learner with the

"Growth Mindset" as someone who knows that his or her abilities and talents can be gained and developed through determination, effort, and the right guidance.

Those with the growth mindset do not always believe everyone shares the same qualities or that everyone can be as "smart as Einstein." However, they do believe that each person has the ability to become more intelligent, talented, and so on, if they make an effort to improve.

Dweck explains that children who were told that they were praised for being "very smart" were more likely to develop a fixed mindset. This may be due to the fact that the children attached the "smart" label to themselves, and therefore sought to maintain this by avoiding any task that might be too difficult for them and therefore make them "look dumb."

On the contrary, children who were praised for doing a good job because they "worked very hard," developed a growth mindset, as this encouraged them to continue to seek solutions to their problems and to learn from their experiences.

Her research further reveals that people with the growth mindset have a higher tendency than those with the fixed mindset to continue to make an effort on a task, regardless of whether there are obstacles or not.

So, with all these in mind, pause to reflect for a moment whether you have been nursing a Fixed Mindset all these years or nurturing a Growth Mindset. Think about the times when you faced a problem in life, or encountered a challenging situation. How did you deal with it?

This would also be a great time to reflect on your beliefs towards your intelligence, habits, and talents. Do you think your current perceptions fall under one mindset or the other? Explore your thoughts and emotions as all the answers that arise would give you clues that can help you unveil your mindset right now.

4 - Embracing the Qualities of a Growth Mindset

Dr. Dweck emphasizes that the ability to succeed is not simply a product of one's talents and abilities, but rather it stems from our belief in ourselves, particularly in our potential to improve. Therefore, we must not be afraid to try and fail, because each experience we go through is essential to our development and, in turn, will help give us a better chance of truly succeeding.

So now that you know how valuable it is to have a growth mindset, you are probably asking yourself, "which strategies can help me and others develop a growth mindset?"

Focus on Learning, not winning

One really simple yet highly effective answer is to change your focus from winning to learning. When you value the process of learning itself, the stress and anxiety you would normally experience from the pressure of winning would diminish in a significant way.

Let us say you are studying for a high-stakes exam. Instead of thinking about how much pressure you are on, how stressed you are, or how embarrassing it would be if you failed, direct your inner speech to ask yourself, "What am I going to learn today?" and "How do I learn it best?"

Aim for Cooperation, rather than Competition

While there is nothing wrong with a little friendly competition every now and then, trouble comes in when it is all you ever think about. The idea that someone else is going to win and you are going to lose can take its toll on you. Instead, concentrate on how you can work with others so that you can achieve your goal in the most efficient and effective way.

For example, if your goal is to run a successful business, concentrate on how you and your team can work so well that you can all deliver the best service you can possibly give to your customers, instead of just focusing on what your competition is all about.

Highlight your Efforts

When you have put a lot of effort into something, always take the time to acknowledge that and then give yourself a pat on the back. Better yet, track your progress so that you can review the results of your hard work over time. This can be highly motivating in itself and will make the overall journey towards your goal more exciting and enjoyable.

In light of this, do be careful on your choice of measuring your progress. For instance, those who aim to get fit sometimes make the mistake of relying solely on the weighing scale to mark their progress when, in fact, some people actually gain weight when they lose excess body fat (because it gets turned into muscle).

Learn to Accept Constructive Criticism

Part of what contributes to a Fixed Mindset is the inability to take in criticism as an opportunity to grow. While there are people out there who make the mistake of throwing mean words at others, there are also those who share really good advice in the form of constructive criticism. It is then up to you to transform their words into something that can help you grow and become even better.

I can be a bit difficult to take in constructive criticism at first, but if you practice with each given opportunity, you will definitely benefit from it. Start by not taking the criticism personally, and instead reflect on it as someone else's observation of your performance.

You can even try to ask for specific details in a polite way so that the person can give you further advice. Finally, thank the person for sharing it with you and let them know that their input will help you do better next time.

Aside from these four strategies, there are plenty of other ways to help you develop a growth mindset, many of which you will learn as you continue to glean from this book.

5 - Building Your Emotional Intelligence and Character

Do you know someone who can control his or her emotions very well? Is that person able to make sensitive and rational decisions even during the most stressful of circumstances?

Most of us know someone whom we admire because of their ability to handle their feelings with grace and, at the same time, understand how other people feel. This person is likely to have what psychologists call "high" Emotional Intelligence. This enables them to maintain good relationships with others, solve problems effectively, and establish a healthy level of self-esteem even during trying times.

With regard to this, would you consider yourself as someone with high Emotional Intelligence? If you are unsure, then what you can do is answer the following questionnaire.

Unveiling your Current Level of Emotional Intelligence

Before you proceed, it is best to grab a pen and paper so you can take note of your answers. For each question, try to give a response from a scale of 1 to 5 first, with 1 being "never," 2 being "rarely," 3 being "occasionally," 4 being "often," and 5 being "highly often." Then, follow it up with a more detailed and descriptive answer.

Are you ready? Let us begin:

1. Have people ever mentioned that you are a good listener?

2. Do you burst out when you start to feel really angry or frustrated at someone or something?

3. Are you able to quickly identify your emotions as soon as you experience them?

4. Do you find your thoughts drifting away when someone else is sharing their thoughts to you?

5. Do you know how to make yourself calm whenever you start to feel anxious or stressed?

6. Do you prefer to work alone rather than to collaborate with other people, especially when they have a different personality than you?

7. Are you fully – or for the most part – aware of your own strengths and weaknesses?

8. Do you find it challenging to let go of a sad or frustrating thought or emotion?

9. Do you find your work or studies enjoyable?

10. When facing a conflict or a situation that calls for a negotiation with other people, do you tend to flee?

11. Do you like to ask other people for their advice on how you can improve on something?

12. Is it challenging for you to identify the kind of emotion another person b is feeling?

13. Do you have goals that you have set for yourself, and do you like to check every now and then how close you are to achieving them?

14. Do you find it difficult to pay attention to someone or something for a long period of time?

15. Are you highly passionate about something, and does it give you the motivation to improve on a certain skill or talent?

16. Is the idea of building rapport with others still a challenge to you?

Once you have finished answering each question, go over each of them and then total the scores for all the odd numbered questions (1, 3, 5, and so on). Then, total all the scores for all the even numbered questions (2, 4, 6, and so on). After that, compare the two sets of scores.

If your score for all the odd numbered questions is significantly higher than for all the even numbered questions, then you are likely to be an emotionally intelligent person. You may have strong and healthy relationships with other people, and you are likely to have great leadership skills.

On the other hand, if your results reveal the opposite, then you may need to focus on enhancing your emotional intelligence. Currently, you might still be struggling with your own emotions and you might be having difficulty handling stress and anxiety. People who are yet to develop their emotional intelligence usually avoid challenges and conflicts.

6 - How to Build Emotional Intelligence

Now that you have a better idea of your current level of emotional intelligence, the best direction for you would be to continue to build upon it.

To help people better understand Emotional Intelligence, Dr. Daniel Goleman, psychologist and New York Times bestselling author of *Emotional Intelligence: Why it can Matter More than IQ* (1996), enumerated its five key characteristics, namely Self-awareness, Self-regulation, Self-Motivation, Empathy, and Social Skills.

Now, here are the ways in which you can work on each of the characteristics so your overall Emotional Intelligence will strengthen over time:

Increase your Self-Awareness

To be self-aware means to be fully aware of your own individual qualities, strengths, and weaknesses. It also means being aware of your emotions as they arise. While we cannot avoid feeling certain negative emotions, such as envy, what we can do is to acknowledge the feeling first and then assess our thoughts rather than to just act upon it.

On the other hand, an example of what is *not* self-awareness is when a person becomes enraged and loses his or her temper, yet denies feeling angry when asked about it. What is worse is when that person denies his or her own anger issues.

To continuously become more self-aware, what you can do is to ask the people you trust would be honest with you about the strengths and weaknesses they see in you. Be prepared to receive both the pleasant and the not so pleasant feedback from them. You might be surprised by some of the qualities they see in you but you were not able to see in yourself.

Exercise Self-Regulation

To exercise self-regulation means to carefully manage your thoughts and emotions before they lead you to do anything you might regret. It also means resorting to some form of exercise in order to help control your emotions.

For example, when you start to feel angry, you would be able to recognize that it *is* anger you are feeling and that you are to breathe in and out deeply to calm yourself, instead of losing your temper. This deep breathing exercise each time you start to feel angry is then considered to be a self-regulation strategy.

There are plenty of other ways for you to exercise self-regulation, and it all depends on which strategies are most effective to you. For example, some people like to write regularly in a journal as a form of catharsis, or the purging of emotional tensions.

Others like to work out regularly to ease any tension and anxiety they feel because of the nature of their work. Some prefer to practice meditation at the start and end of their day to help instill positive thoughts and emotions. You can explore plenty of self-regulation strategies throughout your life, so much so that you can even try a different one each day.

Nurture Empathy

Empathy is defined as the act of not only understanding another's feelings, but also entering it. It is the one referred to by the expression, "putting oneself in someone else's shoes."

In order to truly become emotionally intelligent, one must strive to develop empathy throughout his or her life. One way of learning to become more empathetic is by really listening to another person while he or she is talking. All too often, many of us do not really listen to a friend or a loved one as they share their thoughts and feelings.

Instead, we would try to formulate our own thoughts so that we could share them as soon as the other has stopped talking. Some people do not even wait for the other person to finish, but would interrupt them instead.

If you often find yourself doing this, then the next time you are presented with the opportunity to converse with someone, listen to them wholeheartedly. Notice their emotions and try to see their story from their perspective, instead of through your own lens.

Practice Self-Motivation

Motivation is described as a specific thought that serves as your direction and purpose for acting towards a desired goal. In other words, it is the reason behind your behavior.

Often, we are motivated by external factors, such as continuing to go to work even when it makes us unhappy because we need to earn money to support ourselves and our family. We are motivated to exercise even during the times when we do not feel like it because we want to attain or maintain a healthy body.

However, when we lose our focus from our goal due to our emotions, it can be very hard to be motivated, and only the emotionally intelligent are capable of overcoming such obstacles to remain resilient. It is their self-motivation that enables them to attain their long term goals.

Regardless of what your current level of emotional intelligence is, you are also capable of motivating yourself with the help of many techniques. But while you will indeed learn many of them throughout this book, none of them would work without the key ingredient that is self-discipline.

After all, self-motivation *is* self-discipline, or the ability to convince yourself to do what is right (or what is in line with your goal) in spite of all the distractions.

The good news is that self-motivation or self-discipline is a skill that you can continue to enhance over the years so long as you work at it regularly. Most people find that by starting with easier challenges (such as starting the habit of choosing water over soda) help pave way towards being self-disciplined over harder ones (such as quitting smoking or alcohol).

Try practicing self-motivation on something that is important to you, be it focusing on a particular skill for 1 hour each day, exercising regularly, or controlling your food portions. Over time, you will be able to confidently motivate yourself to do greater things.

Enhance your Social Skills

Good leaders are not those who can come up with the most strategic plans or communicate in the most articulate manner. Rather, they are the ones who have exceptional social skills, or the quality of being able to manage relationships so as to guide others towards a desired path.

Naturally, this requires strategy and convincing words, but without the right people skills, no one would care about your plan or your message.

People with great social skills are those who can easily gain your trust. They are the ones who can establish great rapport with others, handle conflict with grace, effectiveness, and efficiency, and, most of all, remain confident in themselves and in their team.

It goes without saying that the best (if not the only true) way to enhance your social skills is by going out there and socializing with people, especially those whom you are not comfortable with.

By exposing yourself to a lot of interactions and exercising all the other characteristics of Emotional Intelligence, you will be able to notice others' body language, choice of words, and other communicative cues that reveal their thoughts and feelings beyond their words.

Take note that there are no hard and fast "rules" to having great social skills, which is often the reason why some people with high IQ struggle in social settings. That is because these "rules," or tone and volume of voice, body language, and whatnot, are unique to each culture and sub-culture in human society. What may be polite to one culture may be stiff to another.

What is considered to be funny and interesting to one group, may be regarded as rude to the other. Only by enhancing your social skills and paying close attention would you be able to read and understand the ways a sub-culture communicates. Therefore, your ability to adapt and assimilate is the core of having great social skills.

The wonderful thing about working on improving your Emotional Intelligence is it will never end. You have your entire life to continue being more empathetic, self-aware, and motivated to pursue your goals and to help others improve their quality of life as well. There will always be an opportunity for you to strengthen your relationships with loved ones as well as enjoy the pleasure of meeting new people.

Likewise, there will be hurdles along the way, and these are the times when you can practice self-regulation the most. We all go through ups and downs, but with high emotional intelligence we will definitely be able to overcome our limitations and be the master of our own life.

7 - Be More Confident and Unleash Your Hidden Potential

Would you consider yourself to be a fairly confident person? Some would probably say yes, while others would question themselves first. But, no matter how un-confident you may feel right now, rest assured that it is a skill you can learn all by yourself.

Self-confidence is believing in yourself and in your abilities. It is when you jump into a deep pool when you know for a fact that you are a good swimmer, or signing up for a singing competition because throughout your life you have been told your voice is wonderful.

Overall, self-confidence is a positive belief that you are capable of accomplishing what you plan to do. It is so important to have self-confidence in order to succeed and become the master of your life. After all, it is the force that will drive you towards your goal, no matter what.

One thing to keep in mind, though, is that there are two recognized types of self-confidence. According to many psychologists, including Abraham Maslow (the man behind the "hierarchy of needs"), we must learn how to distinguish between the general kind of self-confidence as the quality of one's personality, and the more specific self-confidence, which is in regard to a specific challenge, task, or ability.

We must also come to terms with the different factors that have a direct impact on our level of self-confidence, including our past experiences, our relationships with other people, and our perceived "role" in society.

By taking a step back from all of these and regarding them as if we were a non-participating outsider looking into our own lives, we could realize that we are so much more than what we believe ourselves to be, and that we are fully capable of feeling confident in ourselves and our potential.

Hopefully, at this point you are now ready to learn how to be more confident. So now, let the following sections guide you along the way:

Be Careful Who You Spend Time With

It is a harsh reality to face, but we do have to accept the fact that some people are just not worth losing our self-confidence for. These are the kinds of people who would only say mean things to you or towards others, which in turn can also affect how you feel about yourself.

Some of these types of people might call it "tough love," but if all they ever say to you are "tough" words, then there is certainly no love in that any more.

Of course, this does not mean you should burn your bridges. Rather, you should just spend less time with them and more time with those who share your passions, encourage you, and support you.

Aside from the people in our lives, there is another group of people many of us spend much of our time on, and they are the ones we look up to and listen to regularly.

To you, they could be a celebrity whose television show you watch almost every day, or a famous speaker whose podcast you look forward to during your drive to work, or a creator on YouTube whose videos you binge-watch until the early morning.

Whoever they may be, rest assured they have a huge impact on your life. Consider if this impact is positive or negative, especially with regard to your self-confidence. If you feel that they help you believe in yourself more, then go ahead and continue to learn more from that person.

On the other hand, if he or she makes you feel even more insecure about yourself, then it is about time you move on to someone who can make you feel the exact opposite.

Acknowledge your Achievements

When was the last time you took a moment to reflect on something you did that you are proud of? If you cannot remember, then take this as an opportunity to look back at a time when you felt wonderful, strong, and utterly confident in your abilities.

Let the first memory that comes to mind as soon as you have read that linger for a little while in your thoughts. Try to recall all the details as vividly as you possibly can. How did you feel? What did you say? Why is it such a happy and precious moment to you?

All of us have accomplished something throughout our life, no matter how small that achievement may seem. It is so important to acknowledge what you have done that has made you proud in the past so that you can give yourself the assurance that you are capable of success. It would also be really good for you to express your feelings of gratitude towards that moment and the people that were a part of it.

Now, you can bet that you will be experiencing many other achievements in the future, and so it would be a good idea to capture these moments. You can do that by taking a picture of the moment, or writing about it in your journal.

Some would even write about their achievements along with the date on a small sheet of paper, fold it up, and stuff it into a jar. That way, they can pull one out and read it each time they need a little boost of self-confidence.

Do not be afraid to recognize your feats and to (maybe secretly) revel in them every now and then, especially during times when you feel the least self-confident. After all, these happy times are part of what make life worth living.

Know your Strengths

The word "strength" can mean a lot of things to different people, but in this particular case it refers to an asset of yours that is special and useful to you as well as to others. An example of a "strength" would be a person's cooking skills.

Not everyone knows how to cook well, but if that person does and if it has helped him become successful in life or, at the very least, please the people whom he loves to cook for, then cooking can be regarded as one of his biggest strengths.

Another, less easily measurable example of a strength is being persistent. Let us say you have a group of novices and all of them were challenged to work on a task that they all find equally difficult to do.

In time, some of them might give up sooner than the others. However, it should then make it easy for the last novice, or the one who continues to work on the task no matter how difficult it got, to consider the fact that persistence is one of her biggest strengths.

Now, with regard to this idea of what strengths are, imagine someone coming up to you and asking you what *your* top five biggest strengths are. Would you then be able to tell them straight away? Pause and reflect for a moment the top five strengths you have and then try to recall the moments in your life that made you consider these five qualities in particular.

If you find it a bit difficult to come up with an answer to this question, then it is about time you should get to know your strengths better.

One of the easiest ways to finding out your own strengths is to ask the people who know you best. You can start by telling them that you are trying out this new self-improvement exercise where you need to know your biggest strengths.

Then, ask them if they could tell you one strength of yours that they have noticed. That way, you would not feel like you are fishing for compliments. You would not have to worry if your friend thinks so, too, anyway because good friends support each other in the path to self-improvement.

Another way to find out what your biggest strengths are is by writing them all down. With a pen and paper in hand, ask yourself any of the following questions (or all of them, for that matter):

- What am I good at? What accomplishments in my life am I most proud of?

- What activities make me feel happiest? Why do I like

these particular activities?

- What are my hobbies? How often do I spend time on each hobby?

As your mind churns out answer to each question, just write everything down on the sheet of paper. You can just scribble the words as they come out or you can even doodle them if you prefer to express them in the form of images.

Then, once you are finished, the next thing to do is to peruse your work and then highlight the words – or encircle the images – that you feel are the strongest to you. You can then safely consider these to be your core strengths.

Every effort counts towards making an inventory of your strengths. After all, you can consider them to be your "tools of the trade." For example, if one of your biggest strengths is your ability to communicate well through writing, then perhaps you can challenge yourself write a novel or maintain a blog.

In line with this, you can also continue to strengthen your strengths, and that is by taking up classes and practicing even more to become a master of them. If we go back to the example of your writing skill being one of your strengths, you can consider taking up advanced writing classes or workshops on fiction writing to further enhance your ability to write.

As you can see, the simple act of choosing who and where you spend much of your time on, together with acknowledging your achievements and knowing your strengths, can really change the way you see and believe in yourself.

While your self-confidence will not skyrocket overnight, it become stronger over time as you continue to conscientiously nurture a positive mindset. Start by believing in yourself and what you are capable of right at this very moment, and there is no stopping you from unleashing your true potential.

8 - Design Your Dream Life

Before anything else, let us take some time to appreciate the fact that we still have the rest of our lives ahead of us, a blank canvas that we can freely fill in any way we wish. Feel thankful for all the happy and challenging moments that are now a part of your past, because they filled your days with color.

Now, you have this present opportunity to design the life you have only been dreaming of before. If you already have something in mind – a goal you wish to achieve or a plan you are looking forward to carry out – then let the rest of this chapter help you fill in the rest of the blanks.

On the other hand, if you still need some help in figuring out how you would like to live the rest of your life, then hopefully the following sections will guide you to designing your dream life.

The rest of this chapter will require you to unleash your creative juices, so be ready with some paper, a pen, or perhaps even some coloring materials so you can sketch out your ideas as you read. Begin when you are ready:

Visualize Your Future Self

In this little exercise, you are going to time travel. At least, in your mind's eye. Try to find a quiet space where no one will disturb you for a while, then close your eyes. First, try to picture what life would be like for you three (or five) years from now. Where will you be? What do you look like? How do you feel? Who are you with?

Visualize everything as vividly as you can, including the sights, the smells, the textures, and the emotions of that moment. Does what you see make you feel happy and accomplished? Are you doing the things that you have always wanted to do?

Here is an example of what it is like to visualize your future self:

Let us say that, right now, you are fresh out of school and still in the process of looking for a job. However, as you visualize your future self in your mind's eye, you can see yourself working for your dream company, with your own place and car, with a big savings account, and going on life-changing holiday trips once a month.

You are healthy and fit, because you love working out every

day and you eat healthy, whole foods. You love spending time with your friends and you would have game nights on Fridays, with wine and cheese platters because you have always wanted to do that.

You also see yourself lending out a helping hand to charity organizations that mean so much to you, specifically by helping to get shelter animals adopted by the right families and spending quality time with children at the local orphanage.

As you continue to visualize your future self, try to capture all the most important details on paper. For example, you can sketch out what you look like, write down the name of your dream job, where you will be living, and the make and model of your car, and all the other details you want to take note of.

Once you are finished, you will have filled sheets of paper that you can now use to help you come up with a plan to turn your dream life into a reality.

That being said, be careful not to treat these as if they are set in stone, however, because your visualization of your dream life is merely a guide to keep you motivated and inspired. For instance, the job you might end up with might not be in the company you originally wanted, but it could be even better.

Create Goals that Motivate You

At this point, you should already have your sheets of paper filled with ideas, sketches, and details regarding your dream life. It does not matter if they all look jumbled up right now, because you are now about to transform these dreams into goals.

To do that, what you can do first is get a highlighter and then choose from all of the details the most important one to you. It could be your dream job, having better health, or so on. Once you have highlighted top 1, you move on to top 2, and finally, top 3. The reason why you need to highlight your top 3 is so you will know which ones to prioritize the most if you had to choose.

This does not mean you should let go of the other goals, because if there are times when you do have the opportunity to accomplish them alongside your top 3. However, during moments when you are limited on time and resources, you will be able to tell exactly which tasks you will direct most of your energy to and those are for your top 3 goals.

Now, once you have highlighted your top 3 dreams, the next thing to do is to turn them into goal statements, and to achieve that you can use the SMART acronym as your guide. This was first conceptualized by Peter Drucker, and later re-defined by Professor Robert S. Rubin to help people create real and achievable goals. Simply put, SMART refers to Specific, Measurable, Achievable, Relevant, and Time-based.

For example, if your number one goal based on your dream life visualization exercise is to buy your own house in three years, then you can turn it into a SMART goal by figuring out how you can answer the following questions:

Specific:

- What does your dream house look like?

- Where is it located?

Measurable:

- How much would it cost you to buy/build your dream house?

- How many months/years would it take you to save up

the money to buy/build your dream house?

Achievable:

- Is it possible to be able to save up enough money to buy/build your dream house?

- How will you be able to earn the money you need to buy/build it?

- Relevant:

- How important is it for you to get this dream house?

- How can this dream house contribute to you getting the life you have always dreamed of?

- How relevant is achieving this dream house to your life goals?

Time bound:

- When exactly do you want to buy/build your dream house?

- How many days/months/years is it between now and that date?

Asking yourself these questions might sound a bit tedious, but they will definitely help you put things into perspective and, at the same time, turn your vague goal into something that is highly achievable. You can always do plenty of research and make some adjustments until you know for sure that all your answers to the SMART pointers are realistic, given your current situation.

Once you have the answers, you can then finally turn your goal into a SMART goal. In the example stated, it can sound something like this:

"In three years' time, I will be the owner of a tiny house. It will be made of hardwood and in it, there will be a kitchen, a small bathroom and toilet, a loft bedroom, and a cozy living space.

It will be parked on the empty lot given to me by my parents. It will cost me 50,000 dollars to have someone build it, which means I need to save up 1700 dollars for 30 months so it will be completed by December 1, 2020."

After you have turned each of your top three priorities into SMART goals, you could then proceed to the planning stage, which you will learn about in the next section.

9 - Construct a Detailed Plan to Achieve your Goals

Now that you have your three SMART goals in mind, your next step is to come up with a plan that would enable you to achieve all three of them within the next three years. This will take some time to do, so be prepared to set aside a few hours of your day in order to lay out these plans.

The first step to create a detailed plan for your 1st priority. Write down all of the tasks that need to be done until you are able to achieve that goal. It is not unlike breaking down a large project into smaller, more manageable chunks of tasks that you can tackle day by day.

You can organize the tasks in the form of a to-do list, a progress chart, a diagram, or even a storyboard if you are the artistic type. Just make sure that you can tick off the tasks that you have accomplished so you can proceed to the next one.

If you are unsure of the prerequisites to certain tasks, then you would need to do some research online or make some phone calls until you know exactly what is required.

For example, if one of your goals is to acquire finish law

school in three years, then you will need to know which school you can immediately enroll yourself in, when their next enrollment period is, what is required of you to make you qualified for law school, and so on.

Once you have laid out all the tasks that lead towards your goal, the next step is to create another set for your 2nd goal, and then finally your 3rd goal. Only after you have determined the tasks you need for all three goals should you then create a timetable to carefully plot which tasks for which goals you will need to accomplish on certain months.

You can also color code the "non-negotiable" tasks – or tasks that cannot be rescheduled – so that you can make them your top priority in certain months.

For example, let us say your top 3 goals for the next 3 years are to finish law school, to own a tiny house, and to be able to save up 5,000 dollars after you have saved up the 50,000 for your tiny house. If so, then in your timetable you can highlight the months when you need to really focus on your studies and the months when you can take on extra jobs so you can speed up your savings.

Creating a solid, detailed plan to achieve your goals is definitely not going to be a walk in the park, but it is not rocket science either. Think of it as if you are writing guidelines on how to consistently improve yourself in the next three years.

At the same time, try to have fun in the process. Do not become so overwhelmed by your goals that you forget the reasons why you want to accomplish them in the first place.

How do you feel now that you have a clearer picture of what your dream life is like? Hopefully these activities have inspired you to take charge of your time right now and direct all your energy towards living the life you truly want.

Treat your Body with Care and Respect

Which do you think is more important, good looks or good health? The thing is, most people often worry about their looks when the more important thing to consider is whether they are truly healthy. Besides, when you make sure that your body is healthy, you will always look and feel good.

Unfortunately, many of us often take our body for granted, and it is only during times when we become sick that we realize how important it is for us to take good care of it. Be that as it may, we are all human and therefore we a gentle reminder every now and then to take care of our body.

This is the highest level of respect we can give to our body, and it has a tremendous impact on our self-confidence, happiness, relationship with ourselves and others, and our overall quality of life.

So how do you take good care of your body? The answers have everything to do with our everyday habits, specifically our choice of food, our physical activities, and our ability to manage stress.

While we have heard all about these for so many times already, it does not hurt for us all to take a step back, assess our current lifestyle, and answer the question, "have I been treating my body with care and respect in the last few days (or months?)

Of course, if you already have a system of healthy habits that enable you to maintain a fit and healthy body, then let this chapter serve merely as a source of further motivation and inspiration. On the other hand, if you need some help, then this chapter will definitely point you in the right direction.

That being said, let us move on to the different ways you can take great care of your body to give it the respect it deserves.

Find out how best to nourish your body

We have all heard time and again that we should follow a healthy diet, but what really is the best way to feed our body?

Generally speaking, a "healthy diet" is one that nourishes your body with the right combination of nutrients and fluids to enable it to continue functioning properly. It might seem easy to say that you should have "lots of fruits and veggies" or "more lean protein and less saturated fat," but the truth is it can be a bit more complicated than that.

Think about it: we all have different body types and we all do different activities every day, which means each of us has a unique set of requirements to maintain a healthy body. In other words, what might be a good dietary program for you might actually be harmful to someone else.

Thus, the best solution should be to consult a reliable pro-fessional, such as a registered dietitian, so that you can find out exactly how you can best nourish your body.

If you think only rich people can afford to talk to a professional, let go of your fears. Consulting a registered dietitian is very much worth the investment because his or her professional advice can help lead you to a healthier body and save your life someday.

For instance, some people did not even know they were eating foods that were actually harmful to them until a professional explained it to them. Then, by removing those foods from their diet, many of the symptoms they used to experience disappeared. Moreover, they were finally able to attain their much desired healthy body weight.

To find the right registered dietitian, you can start by asking your trusted family and friends to refer one to you. You can also look up online to find one in your area and then do a bit of background research on him or her on blogs, forums, and so on.

You can even give his or her office a call before you drop by so that you would not only be able to schedule an appointment, but also find out what you need to prepare before your visit.

It would also be a good idea to keep a food log a few days or weeks before your scheduled visit. This will help the registered dietitian to find out exactly how he or she can help you. Aside from this, you should take note of all your past illnesses, allergies, and other symptoms you have experienced.

If you experience this often, your registered dietitian will most likely work hand in hand with a physician to diagnose any underlying health problems you may have. Then, he or she can prescribe to you the best diet for treatment and prevention.

Let your body explore what it is capable of

Do you love to exercise? If you do not, then it simply means you have not discovered the kind of physical activities that excite you. Physical exercise is vital to our overall health, not just in order to maintain a fit physique, but to boost the immune system, enhance our stamina, slow down aging, and a host of other benefits.

In fact, some of the most successful people in the world dedicate a specific amount of their time each day to exercise – regardless of how "busy" they are – because they know it is one of the biggest investments they could ever make.

One example would be former U.S. President Barack Obama, who mentioned in his autobiography, *Dreams From My Father,* that he used to be an underachiever until he began running for three miles daily.

Likewise, Facebook CEO Mark Zuckerberg makes it a point to work out at least thrice weekly. He also explained that being physically fit gives you more energy, and thus this will enable you to do more and do them well.

Now you might think that someone like Anna Wintour, the Editor-in-Chief of American Vogue, would be too busy to make time for exercise. On the contrary, she is known for waking up at 5:45 in the morning so she could play tennis. She explained that doing so helps her strengthen her willpower and focus on moving forward.

Now, if these famous and really successful people still make sure to find time to exercise, why can't we? After all, it would be a shame to let our bodies wither away without exploring what they are truly capable of. Absolutely no money is required if you set aside even just 10 to 20 minutes of your day doing jumping jacks, sit ups, or go on a quick run around the block.

All of these will keep your metabolism up and will give you a natural surge of energy and positive emotions that can help boost your self-confidence and can-do attitude for the rest of the day.

At this point, you are probably wondering how you can motivate yourself to work out. Well, truth be told it can be a bit of a challenge sometimes. If it were not, we would all be able to wake up early and exercise regularly. So, to help you out, here are some tips on how you can motivate yourself unleash your body's full potential through the habit of exercise:

Make exercise as easy as 1 2 3 to start

The more convenient it is to start doing something, the more likely you are to just get up and do it, and the same general idea applies to exercise. For instance, if the idea that it takes you an hour's drive to the gym and then another hour to drive back home discourages you from working out, then ditch the gym and work out at home instead. The only exception to this is if you absolutely love working out at the gym.

Another way to make exercise easier to start is by preparing everything well in advance. For example, if the only time you can spare for exercise is in the early morning, then you can make it easier for yourself to begin the next day by laying out all of your workout clothes on a chair close to your bed the night before.

That way, you will have eliminated the task of preparing for your workout and you can proceed directly to exercise.

Designate a workout space in your home.

The fastest and easiest way to make exercise an essential part of your lifestyle is to assign a place for it in your home. No matter how small your apartment is, you can always find a means to exercise in it. For instance, you can make use of the hundreds of standing exercise video tutorials on the internet.

Building a workout space at home does not mean you should buy all sorts of equipment as well. Maybe you can create a collection of free weights and other such tools later on, but for the meantime you can actually exercise with nothing but the clothes you are wearing on your back. Just search for any "no equipment needed" exercises online and you are sure to find a guide to help you out.

Some people would even surround their home with motivational cues to remind themselves regularly to get fit. You can frame a printed quotes to inspire you to continue to take good care of your body. Here are some suggestions:

- "The purpose of training is to tighten up the slack, toughen the body, and polish the spirit." – Morihei Ueshiba

- "If you push me towards a weakness, I will turn that weakness into a strength." – Michael Jordan

- "You can't get much done in life if you only work on the days when you feel good." – Jerry West

- "Do not let what you cannot do interfere with what you can do." – John Wooden

- "There may be people that have more talent than you, but there's no excuse for anyone to work harder than you do." – Derek Jeter

- "You can motivate by fear, and you can motivate by

reward. But both those methods are only temporary. The only lasting thing is self motivation." – Homer Rice

- "I am building a fire, and every day I train, I add more fuel. At just the right moment, I light the match." – Mia Hamm

Add variety to your workouts

Doing the same thing every day can get really boring to most people, so if you feel the same way, you should try a different workout every day. Aside from the fact that there are literally thousands of workout videos you can try from the internet, there are also plenty of different classes you can sign up to. You can try Zumba dancing, Pilates, spin class, hip hop, weight training... the list goes on.

It also helps to find out which workouts best suit your personality type. For example, if you are more of an extroverted type of person (or one who gains energy when you are spending time with other people), then you are more likely to enjoy exercises as part of a group.

On the other hand, introverts (or people who regain their

energy from spending time alone) might prefer to do solo exercises, such as running along a trail, swimming, or at-home workouts.

With all these in mind, you can start working out straight-away. Try not to over plan your workout or overthinking the idea of working out, because in reality what matters is you get up and do it. And when you do it every day, your body will become stronger, faster, and even more resilient.

10 - Allow yourself to get enough rest each night

There is no denying it: sleep is an integral piece of the puzzle if you aim to take good care of your body. Regular quality sleep replenishes your energy, protects your mental health, and refreshes your overall well-being. In fact, getting enough rest each night will significantly improve your energy levels and focus every morning. This is especially important if you have got a lot of tasks to do on busy days.

There are plenty of strategies for those who often find it difficult to go to bed and get enough sleep each night. If you happen to be one of them, then here are some of them to help you out:

Avoid caffeine at least 8 hours before bedtime.

This might sound like a hard thing to do, especially if you are working on a particularly challenging task. However, it takes at least 6 hours and 30 minutes for caffeine to be eliminated from your bloodstream, so if you had your coffee or soda in less time than that before you go to bed, you would find it really difficult to fall asleep.

For example, let us say you are the kind of person who requires at least 6 hours and 30 minutes of sleep every day, but you have to be up at exactly 6 a.m. to prepare for work. That means you need to be asleep on or before 11:30 in the evening each night, and thus you should avoid taking caffeine in any form after 3:00 p.m.

There are plenty of great alternatives to caffeine if you are looking for an instant surge of energy. The easiest and healthiest would be fresh fruit, because their high sugar content can increase your blood sugar levels and give you that push.

If you are pre-diabetic or diabetic, however, it is best to avoid anything too sugary. So, you should instead resort to warm drinks that are both healthy and contain zero carbohydrates, such as ginger, peppermint, green, or chamomile tea.

Surprisingly, exercise in the early morning can also be a great alternative to coffee's energy boost. That is because it can increase your metabolism and boost blood flow to the brain.

Moreover, it will trigger the release of endorphins, or the

hormones that improve your mood. As a result, you will not only have better energy and stamina for you to do your tasks well, but you will also have a much more positive mindset towards them.

Maintain a quiet, dark, and cool bedroom

A bedroom that is clean, fresh, cool, and dark is the ideal place in which to sleep. If you cannot describe your bedroom as any of these, then it is highly likely the reason why you put off or find it difficult to sleep each night. We spend over 200 thousand hours of our life asleep, after all, so why not invest in making it a great experience?

You do not have to break the bank to make your bedroom a great sleep sanctuary. For instance, you can start by hanging thicker curtains if lights from outside keep you from falling asleep.

You can also give your pillows (or your mattress, for that matter) a decent upgrade if the lumps have been bothering you for quite some time now. You can also play some relaxing music or a lulling audiobook to help you fall asleep at night, if the silence or background noise distracts you.

It might also help you to know that the ideal temperature for optimal sleep is between 60 and 67 degrees F. However, if turning on the AC each night proves to be too hard on your utility budget, there are other ways in which you can cool down your room.

For instance, you can sleep on cotton sheets, use an electric fan with the windows open, and wear cool and breathable clothes. It also helps to take a warm shower before bed, so that when you enter your cooler bedroom your body temperature will decrease slightly and help you get a little bit drowsy.

Journal before you go to bed

Most people, especially the busy ones, find it hard to fall asleep at night because they have too much going on in their minds. Unfortunately, all that worrying will do nothing but worsen the situation because then it will cause sleep deprivation and negatively impact their mood in the following day.

If constant worrying at night is what keeps you up, then one simple but effective solution is to write out all of your thoughts in your journal. By transferring them from your head to paper, you are making your abstract worries more tangible and thus more solvable.

You can create to-do lists, draw diagrams, or sketch out your thoughts and plans so you can rest assured that you have a solution and can deal with it in the morning. That being said, it is best to journal on actual paper instead of on a digital device, because the blue light from your smart-phone or laptop will keep you awake.

Try to use a lamp with a warm light so that it will still en-able you to fall quickly to sleep after you have finished your journaling.

It is plain to see that our body does not require an elaborate plan, complicated tools, and expensive systems for you to be able to take really good care of it.

By following the best dietary plan for you, exercising regu-larly, and ensuring quality sleep every time, you are already respecting it. In return, your body will be able to perform at its best and you will be able to master your mindset and live the kind of lifestyle you truly want.

11 - Destroy Negative Energy through Self Love

The issue with society's perception of self-love is its association with excessive pride and interest in one's self. As a result, most people think people who love themselves are egocentric, vain, and selfish. However, it is self-love that allows you to show yourself the same kind of love and respect that you have for others. In the process, your self-confidence, self-esteem, and positive energy will grow.

Those who find it difficult to love themselves are also the ones who tend to listen to a negative inner voice in their minds telling them they are not good enough. If you consider yourself to be one of them, then this chapter will show you how to destroy that negative energy and embrace yourself for who you are right now.

Bring Your Negative Beliefs to the Surface

It is sad to think that many children grew up in a place where the adults or their peers constantly point out their flaws and criticize everything they do. Sometimes, these children grow up believing in all the negativity, so much so that their own mind becomes their worst critic.

Unless they decide to overcome these negative beliefs, they will wake up each day to a pessimistic mindset that will hold them back from achieving their full potential.

More often than not, many who have negative beliefs about themselves are not actually aware of it. That is because negative thinking has always been their version of reality. If you yourself are unsure of whether you see through pessimistic lens most of the time, try to find out if any of these statements ring true to you:

- You always worry about most things and you find it difficult to let go of your anxious thoughts.

- Your favorite quote is Murphy's Law: "whatever can go wrong, will go wrong."

- You find it difficult to socialize with other people because you fear that what you say to them can be used against you in some way.

- Each time you hear good news, your mind always manages to put a negative spin to it. For instance, if a friend tells you she just got engaged, you immediately entertain thoughts that nothing lasts forever.

- You find yourself constantly complaining, whether it is about the weather, your job, bad luck, or the people you deal with every day.

- You love to stay in your comfort zone and you avoid trying out new things whenever possible.

- You are crippled by the thought of failure. Because you always want things to be perfect, you try to avoid doing anything that you are not already good at.

- When someone assigns you to work on a project, you immediately thing it is not going to work out as planned.

If these statements are the exact opposite of who you are, then you can take a moment to feel grateful for already being a positive person. On the other hand, if you cannot help but agree with these statements, breathe a sigh of relief that you are being honest with yourself and that you are taking the steps towards changing your mindset.

12 - Overcome Cognitive Distortions

Thankfully, there are ways to identify which thoughts actually have a negative impact on your mindset. Psychologists call these negative thoughts "cognitive distortions," and they are the core reasons why some people continue to have a negative and fixed mindset.

You can try to observe your own inner speech and see if you can catch any the common cognitive distortions below. Then, try the solutions that follow so you can help yourself in overcoming them:

Personalization

This is the idea that you are the reason for something to happen or for someone to be acting in a certain way. People who personalize also tend to take responsibility for a certain event even though in reality there is no direct connection between it and them.

Example: *She did not smile and greet me today like she usually does. I surely must have done something to upset her.*

Heaven's Reward Fallacy

The thought that all the pain, sacrifice, and bitterness you are experiencing will lead you to a sweet reward later on. However, when that expected reward does not come, you could end up feeling worse.

Example: *Even though my partner is physically and emotionally abusive, I know I will be rewarded for continuing to be faithful and loyal in this relationship.*

Blaming

The habit of always managing to find someone else to blame each time you encounter a difficult situation. Sometimes when you think you are the one to blame, you feel terrible about it, so you sometimes end up punishing yourself.

Example: *If my co-worker had been more careful, I would not be in this stupid position right now. This is all his fault!*

Mislabeling

The concept of associating yourself and others with a particular quality or, in other words, labeling yourself and others as if the quality is your/their identity. For instance, just because you failed a math test in high school does not mean you will always "suck at math."

Example: *I know I'm going to embarrass myself in front of these people again, just like I've always done. I'm such a failure.*

Black and White Thinking

This mindset believes that there is no such thing as a "gray area," because everything is an all or nothing situation. If they do not get what they want, they would feel devastated about it.

Example: *It does not matter if I pass this exam or not, because if I don't get to be top one, I might as well consider myself a total failure.*

Catastrophizing

People who tend to have this form of negative thinking believe that things will always turn out for the worst. Each time something bad happens, they would magnify it, often to the point of hopelessness.

Example: *No matter how well they planned it, this party is not going to turn out well at all, especially since it's about to rain.*

Filtering

People who harbor this type of thinking pattern tend to only look at the negative aspects of a given situation because they filter out the benefits. They also would focus too much on their "flaws" or "weaknesses" as well as compare themselves to others often.

Example: *I hate my fat body, my pimples, and my frizzy hair. Why can't I look like her, instead? This is so unfair.*

"Should" thinking

This cognitive distortion is common among those who grew up in a rather strict environment. They tend to be worrisome and uptight, often finding it difficult to handle personalities who do not always conform to the "rules."

Example: *We should always follow the rules. Anyone who is not should be severely punished.*

Thinking negatively about yourself and/or others is not uncommon, but that does not mean you should not do something about it. These cognitive distortions and many others are often the reason why people hold themselves back from achieving their goals in life. They continue to make up excuses, feel sorry for themselves, and hide within their comfort zones because they have become so used to it.

To overcome these cognitive distortions, the first thing you should do is to acknowledge to yourself that you do resort to cognitive distortions during stressful situations. It takes great courage to be honest with yourself sometimes, but it will really help you to acknowledge that your negative thoughts are becoming a problem and that you want to do something about them.

Another strategy that often works is to question them. To do that, memorize any of the following questions so you can easily bring them up as soon as your inner speech conjures them:

- Am I being too hard on myself?

- Is this a fact, or is this just my Negative Self talking to me again?

- Is this within my control?

  - If it is... what is one good thing I can do about it?

  - If it is beyond my control, then what can I learn

from it?

- Should I take this thought seriously?

- Why did I think that? What led me to think that way?

This takes lots of practice on self-awareness, but if you always have them, then you will have plenty of opportunities to practice and get better.

A really important tip to remember when you notice that your negative thoughts are becoming overwhelming is to identify your top 3 common sources of stress. Consider the factors in your life right now that are causing you to feel more stressed, demotivated, and more in a rut than usual.

It could have something to do with your job, your personal relationships, or your current lifestyle. Whatever they are, identify them and then think about how you can free yourself from them. If they are factors beyond your control, then consider how you can cope with them in a more productive, healthy, and positive way.

By being self-aware of these negative thought patterns and then proactively exercising the solutions to overcome them, you will be able to break out of your shell, learn to truly love yourself, and unleash your full potential.

Let Go of Perfectionism

Many of us grew up believing that, in order for us to survive in this world, we have to be the best, brightest, most talented... The list goes on. As a result, many of us have become perfectionists who have set almost impossibly high standards for ourselves as well as for others.

You can tell whether you are suffering from perfectionism if you are never fully satisfied with your work, if you constantly blame yourself if something did not work out the way you want it to, and if you always size yourself – and others – up against those whom you believe have it more than you do.

Another thing is that perfectionists often avoid situations in which they might make mistakes, mostly because they have associated them with a failed life. If you feel the same way, do consider the fact that mistakes are part of the learning process and that everyone, especially the most successful people on earth, experiences failure and rejection multiple times throughout life.

It is also interesting to note that a prevalent bad habit

among perfectionists is chronic procrastination, and the reason for this is that they are afraid they would not be able to do the task flawlessly. Perfectionists are highly critical of themselves, so much so that their self-confidence and self-worth rely on how successful, accomplished, or attractive they are.

All these qualities caused by perfectionism make perfection-ists prone to a wide range of mental disorders, including anxiety disorders, depression, and even eating disorders in the case of those who are obsessed with their appearance.

If your mindset is heavily influenced by the idea that everything has to be perfect, it is time to break out of it and free yourself. Perfectionism may be one of the core reasons that is holding your back from truly loving yourself and al-lowing yourself to experience what life has to offer, so you are definitely much better off without it.

When you are ready, here are some great strategies on how you can break out of the limitation of perfectionism and start working on your goals in life:

Understand your "Why"

As mentioned earlier, perfectionists tend to procrastinate

on even the important tasks because they fear they would not be able to do it perfectly right away. Sometimes, they would procrastinate on activities that could possibly "help" make the situation "perfect" for them so as they can work on the task as flawlessly as possible.

For instance, they would make themselves a cup of coffee, clean and organize their work space, and so on, as if all these things could lead them to taking action on the most important task.

While there is nothing wrong with enjoying coffee or keeping a neat and tidy workspace, neither of these actually lead towards accomplishing the real goal. Wasting time on other things besides the one really important task is the worst thing anyone can possibly do, so much worse than doing it haphazardly.

So, if your procrastination has been causing you to procrastinate on something, one thing you can do next time to spur you to action is this: think of the reason why finishing this task is so important to you. Give yourself 3 to 5 minutes to drill into your mind that "done" is better than "perfect."

The next time you are tempted to procrastinate on an important task. Try asking yourself, "Why do I need to get this done? Why is it so important for me to finish this task, perfect or not?"

By focusing on finishing the task, you will be able to do it right away. Only after it has been completed should you then go right ahead and polish it as perfectly as you want it to be.

Accept that You Cannot Control Everything

Being obsessed with perfection, perfectionists have the desire to take control of each and every aspect of their life. However, there are definitely many areas that no one has complete control over. Some perfectionists find this difficult to understand, which is why they often end up blaming themselves.

For instance, all of us have absolutely no control over the physical features bestowed upon us by nature. In fact, they can simply be regarded as a combination of genes passed down to you through your parents.

However, some people would blame themselves for having

such physical features that cause them to believe they are unconventionally attractive. As a result, they are at risk of developing Body Dysmorphic Disorder (BDD), or an obsessive dislike of certain aspects of one's appearance.

To overcome the constant need for control, what you can do is to surrender it all by accepting everything for what it is. Ask yourself, "Is this within my control?" If you can honestly admit that it is beyond your control, then gently remind yourself that you can accept it and let it go.

By letting go of the negative energy and finding the time to truly reconnect with yourself, you would be able to discover and appreciate some aspects of you that you never noticed before. Do not for one second give up on yourself and your individuality, because no matter what happens you can always find something to be grateful for in your life.

However, if, no matter how much you try, you simply find it too much of a challenge to be able to love and appreciate yourself, then do not hesitate to seek help from others. Ask a family member or a close friend to help you, and together you can both seek a therapist you can trust.

We all do need the support of others sometimes, and when

life gets a little bit too rough, rest assured there is someone who can lift you up and inspire you to love yourself.

Build and Maintain a System of Smart Habits

"We are what we repeatedly do. Excellence, then, is not an act, but a habit."

Such a powerful message was shared over two thousand years ago by Greek philosopher Aristotle and then eloquently relayed by U.S. writer Will Durant in his 1926 book, "The Story of Philosophy."

To this day, these words ring true, because much of who we are now and what we are experiencing is a result of all the habits we have acquired through the years. Therefore, it goes without saying that our mindset and, consequently, our lifestyle is made up of a combination of habits.

For the record, a habit is defined by psychologists as an "automatic pattern of behavior" that serves as a reaction to a specific situation. There is much debate as to whether a habit can be inherited genetically, but one thing is for certain, and it is that many of our habits are acquired through repetition.

The big question, though, is not how a habit works or how it forms, but whether we can honestly consider most of your habits to be "good" or "smart." Better yet, we should ask ourselves whether or not our habits are helping us get closer to achieving our goals in life.

Go ahead and reflect on how you have been spending your time these past few days. You can even grab a pen and paper so you can jot down all the little habits you have been keeping for a while now. If you are not sure of how you can define a particular behavior of yours as a habit or not, what you can do is to count how many hours in a day you are awake, and then identify the different ways you allocate those hours.

Let us say you usually wake up at 8 in the morning. What are the things you usually do right after that, and how much time do you spend on each activity?

Through this exercise, people often realize they spend too much time on social media or doing things that are unrelated to their goals. If you feel the same way, then this self-awareness is the perfect opportunity for you to get out of that rut and take control over your time and behavior.

In short, you need to build a system of smart habits. Of course, that is easier said than done, but the following sections are going to help you overcome your bad habits so you can start building the ones that are going to bring you closer to your dream life.

13 - Identify the Habit Trigger

Right now, think of a habit you already have.

Once you have got that habit in mind, try to trace back the situation right before it that leads you to doing that habit. That situation is called the "habit trigger," and it is your key to breaking a bad habit and starting a good one.

For instance, if a person has the bad habit of spending too much time on social media, he should determine what triggers him to go on social media in the first place. First, he can try to trace back to the last thought and/or action before he launches his social media.

Maybe seeing his phone makes him think about checking his social media, or maybe it is the idea that he might be missing out on something. Whatever his habit trigger is, he should change it so that it will no longer lead him to the habit he wants to eliminate.

Let us say this person realizes he checks his social media each time he sees the icons on his phone. And the reason why he checks his phone is so he could check the time, but now this has automatically led him to check his social media as well. Therefore, it is safe to say that the thought of checking his time on his phone is what triggers him to check his social media.

Now, to stop his social media habit, what he can do is to use his wristwatch instead of his phone to check the time. He can also uninstall his social media apps on his phone so that it would be a bit more difficult for him to check for updates each time he checks the time on his phone.

As you can see, breaking a bad habit gets easier once you have identified its trigger. Of course, it will require some willpower to break bad habits that you actually love, but if you know for a fact that they are not in line with your big goals in life, then the effort you put into eliminating them will be much worth it.

Start Easy but Consistently

The only way to really get rid of a bad habit is to replace it with a good one. Otherwise, if you try to just "remove" the bad habit, the temptation of doing it again would be too strong.

On the other hand, attempting to trump a big bad habit with an equally big good habit is going to be a challenge, especially if the former is much easier and more convenient to do than the latter.

Instead, what you can do is to think about a really easy good habit that you can use to replace your bad habit with. Then, practice that good habit as consistently as you can.

For example, if you want to build the smart habit of exercising every day but the thought of going to the gym discourages you from even starting, you can opt to do something much easier, such as a quick and simple 5-minute exercise at home. Sure, it might not get you to burn off as many calories as a 45-minute workout at the gym, but at least you are *actually* going to do it consistently.

In time, you will find the 5-minute exercise to be so easy that it becomes "automated" into your system. Then, you will find yourself adding more minutes to it, until you realize your habit has become an entire 45-minute workout at home.

The bottom-line is that taking the quick and easy route is always better than planning a big and ambitious route that you are never really going to take anyway. So, start easy and work your way from there.

Sustain your Self-Control

Starting a smart habit can be fun, but even a person with

really good self-discipline is prone to skipping certain days. The only difference between them and the rest, though, is that they always manage to get themselves back on track *right away.*

It is crucial to get back on your habit as soon as possible, otherwise you could start to develop the bad habit you had replaced it with. Some people find this hard to do, especially those who suffer from perfectionism. However, you must not dwell on your mistakes because what really matters is the long-term progress.

Let us say you have been building the habit of exercise in the last 3 weeks, when one day you wake up and felt so lazy you could not bring yourself to even do 10 jumping jacks.

By the end of the day, you realized you had not worked out at all, so you feel sorry for yourself. That, however, does not mean you should give up on your goal of building the exercise habit altogether. Rather, you should pick yourself up, brush yourself off, and decide then and there that you are going to exercise again tomorrow.

So, the next time you make a mistake, such as falling into a bad habit or forgetting to follow through with a smart one, be patient with yourself. Do not magnify your mistakes. What is done is done, but let that not ruin the potential of what you can still do now.

Now that you have learned these tips on how to build a smart system of habits, the only thing left for you to do is to implement them straightaway! Take note that takes a great deal of willpower and several days (or even months) of repetition before a behavior becomes "automated" into your life. So, the sooner you start, the sooner your desired behavior becomes a habit.

Motivate Yourself to Stop Planning and Start Doing

As you continued to learn about how your mindset works, read up on ways to overcome your limitations, create goals that make up your dream life, design a system of smart habits, and lay out all the plans to help you get to where you want to be, you probably felt really productive and ready to jumpstart your life.

While it cannot be denied that planning is a crucial part of the process, it is unfortunate that many people remain stuck in the planning and never get to the most important part:

the doing.

Now, do not beat yourself up for taking too much time to plan when you know for a fact you should start taking action. But if you cannot seem to bring yourself out of the comfort zone of making to-do lists, designing diagrams, and rereading the same self-help guides over and over again, then this chapter will help you motivate yourself to go out there and walk the talk:

Do Not Overthink the Plan

Stop trying to think of a grand plan that can save you from procrastinating on an important task. Instead, make yourself get up and do it. There is no such thing as the "perfect weather" for exercise, or the "best" time for writing your novel, or the "ideal" diet to help you lose weight. Just start doing it today and then work your way from there.

Sometimes, it also helps to not over plan certain things. Of course, you should definitely still have an overview of what you want to achieve and how you can get there, but try not to get too detailed about it. That is because adding too many details to a plan can cause you to believe that it is too complicated. As such, you could end up procrastinating on the plan.

Time Your Planning Session

If you always catch yourself sitting down for hours with a pen and paper, designing the most elaborate plans that could get you to your goal, what you can do to prevent that in the future is to time these sessions.

You can try setting your timer to 10 minutes when you are in the mood to plan. Then, as soon as you hear the timer, work on what you have already planned out and do not add any more to it until you have actually accomplished what is already on your plan.

Reward Yourself only after a Done Job

If you want to condition your mindset to love the doing part more than the planning part, try depriving yourself of what makes you feel good – be it the latest episode of your favorite television series or a nice hot cup of latte – until you have actually finished the important task of the day. That way, you will be more inclined to work on the task than to just plan or procrastinate.

You can also ask help from a family member or friend to

hold off your reward until you can submit proof that you have accomplished your major task. For instance, you can let your roommate set the password to your Wi-Fi and then tell them not to let you know until you can prove that you have finished adding a new chapter in your novel.

You can even create a reward system for your set of tasks. For example, you can pin a picture of a pair of trendy running shoes that you have always wanted to buy on your corkboard.

Then, right below it you can add a checklist of the number of runs per day you have to complete before you can reward yourself with those shoes. After each run, tick off another day so you can actually track your progress and at the same time, notice that you are getting closer to your reward.

There are plenty of other techniques to help you start doing what you have set out to do. But even if there are no shortcuts or magical elixirs that will boost your self-motivation, you can still manage to bring yourself to do it as long as you remember that the doing is what really makes history. So, go out there and work on your goals. After all, the only worst thing you can do is to do nothing at all!

14 - Conclusion

Are you ready to overcome your limitations and live your dream life?

Now that you have now reached the end of this book, the next step for you is to put everything into action.

Keep in mind that nothing big ever comes easy, so take it one day at a time to master your mindset and adopt a healthier and more positive attitude towards yourself and your life.

Take care not to fall into the negative mindset again by continuing to take good care of yourself and by creating little reminders to help keep your motivated and energized. However, do not be too hard on yourself if the going gets tough.

Instead, go on a little retreat to help you sort out your priorities, refresh your mind, and relax your body. That way, you can get back to building your skills and conquering life's challenges. Of course, can always go back to the chapters here that really inspire you and help you to get back on track.

So, go ahead and start mastering your mindset today and grant yourself the power to take back your life and live it the way you have always wanted!

Book 4 - Analyze People

A Power Course To Instantly Analyze Anyone (Body Language, Psychology, Social Mastery, Personal Growth)

1 - Introduction

I want to thank you and congratulate you for buying the book.

This book contains various ways to analyze people, from their facial expressions to their body languages, to their personality traits and temperaments, to their interests and preferences.

The goal is to arm you with tools, perspectives, frameworks, and examples for readers like you to gain a deeper understanding and appreciation of your fellow beings, and in the process, foster more constructive and positive interactions.

Thanks again for buying this book. I hope you enjoy and learn something from it to help you navigate the social world better.

2 - Why Should We Learn How to Read People Better?

"Life is about running your own car as it was built to be run, plus getting along with the other drivers on the highway."

—Elsie Lincoln Benedict and Ralph Paine Benedict, lecturers and writers

It is human nature to seek to navigate the world better. This means knowing what makes people tick, both ourselves and other people.

If we think of ourselves as cars or motorcycles cruising along the road of life, it means knowing what types of engines or motors we have, what makes our engines run, knowing the rules and road signs, taking cues from other vehicles that we pass by, and putting these all together to help us navigate and reach our destinations or goals.

With this book as our roadmap, let us take the journey along the tricky and scenic roads of social navigation.

3 - The Human Alphabet

Imagine looking at a page in a book, and just seeing some funny little marks and symbols, but not being able to make sense of any of it. Imagine looking at people opening and closing their mouths, producing some random sounds, but just hearing gibberish.

We are like this when we were babies. Then, we uttered our first word, took our first step, read our first word, and learned the 26 letters of the alphabets and its combinations, and our world wasn't the same again.

Now, imagine going through the world, interacting with people, but not able to really understand what they are telling you and what they are not telling you. Or assuming you understand them, but then it turns out you don't, hurting feelings and sensibilities in the process, or coming across as presumptuous or ignorant.

Despite our extensive education, elaborate social network, and technological advancements, we still have much to learn about how to read people better. This is because humans are complex, multi-dimensional, and constantly evolving.

Reading people is an intricate endeavor, but not impossible.

Experts have formulated frameworks and conducted studies that analyze human behavior. Moreover, though humans have a lot of differences and idiosyncrasies, we also have similarities and commonalities.

As Elsie Lincoln Benedict and Ralph Paine Benedict said in their book How to Analyze People on Sight, reading people is essentially about learning the human alphabet and its combinations that make each person unique despite having similar basic blueprints.

As a caveat, though Elsie and Ralph's book was published way back 1921, its premises still hold true and relevant in this modern age, and we will refer to this book liberally in this chapter.

The Power of Self-Awareness

The key to understanding people, first and foremost, is understanding yourself. With self-awareness and self-understanding as your anchors, you are in better position to understand people better. You get to understand how different and how similar they are to you. You determine how to deal with them appropriately without losing your cool or yourself.

As you read this book, examine yourself via-à-vis, other people. Remember that communication is a two-way thing. What aspects of yourself are you projecting to other people? How do your words and actions affect other people's words and actions? These are just some points to consider and ponder upon as we go along.

The Power of Non-Verbal Communication

Another key to understanding people is to hear what they say and what they leave unsaid. In his 1971 book Silent Messages, Psychologist Albert Mehrabian concluded that communication is 93% non-verbal and 7% verbal. Specifically, the 93% is broken down into 55% visual or facial and body language and 38% vocal or intonation.

While Albert's findings were based on business presentations and while there are some criticisms on the conclusions, the findings make sense in ordinary interactions.

For instance, have you ever wondered why we tend to forget the names of the people we just met, but remember random things about them like their footwear? Have you ever considered that non-verbal language such as smiles, laughter, and facial expressions are more universal than the English language?

Evolutionary Significance of Reading People

Our ancestors are experts in reading the environment. As hunter-gatherers, they know the best time and the best place to hunt for food. They know the exact moment when to attack. They know when not to attack. They know when an animal is ready to attack, and these signal a fight-or-flight response in them. They know if a plant is edible or poisonous.

Without maps and navigation apps, they navigated forests, mountains, and seas using the sky and surroundings. They know when to expect rain, storm, sometimes even earth-quakes.

Fast forward to our modern world, our environment has changed. For the most part, we have turned aside our hunter-gatherer skills for more technology-related and in-formation-focused competencies.

However, as Elsie and Ralph pointed out, the setting has

changed but the game remains the same. It is still survival of the fittest. But instead of Mother Nature, we are now dealing with human nature.

Like our ancestors, we need to understand our environment, because when we understand better, we act better.

In this modern world, we rely heavily on other people to survive and thrive. Behind every product you use and every service you avail of are people. We also deal with people on a more personal and intimate level. We have our relationships and connections: families, friends, colleagues, significant other.

Understanding people with keen and accurate insight, as well as with kindness and thoughtfulness, can help avoid hurting feelings, trespassing or invading personal spaces, making wrong assumptions and misinformed decisions, and unnecessarily or even unintentionally burning bridges.

4 - Debunking Some Misconceptions on Reading People

Reading people has its share of bad reputation and misconceptions. Maybe you yourself have some of these notions embedded in your conscious and subconscious mind. It pays to visit and address these misconceptions now to prevent cognitive dissonance or conflicting thoughts later.

Misconception #1: Reading people is judging and putting them in boxes.

While it is true that reading people entails making some judgment calls and trying to understand people using our existing mental boxes, the process is more complex than simply judging and putting people in boxes.

It is the difference between reading people and judging intention. Between putting in boxes and thinking outside the box, intuition. Reading people is a creative and active process that has good intentions, which is to understand people, and has good intuition, which is to acknowledge boxes but be willing to go beyond boxes and even change the boxes when necessary.

Psychologist Barbara Markway, Ph.D. said that judging

people does not define them, rather, it defines you. Judging is close-ended and does leave room for doubt or growth. So strive instead to understand people.

When we read people, we seek to understand them, not to judge or change them, but so we can react and act appropriately around them. It is an exercise of intention and intuition. In seeking to know our fellows more, we also hone ourselves.

Misconception #2: Reading people is limiting.

In line with the notion that reading people is putting people in boxes, there is also the belief that it is limiting.

But once we acknowledge that reading people goes beyond judging, we then realize that it broadens our horizon instead of limiting it, that it not just makes us empowered, but also sets the stage for empowering the people we seek to understand.

Misconception #3: Reading people is manipulative.

Some people shy away from reading people because they do not want to be judging and manipulative. But remember, it is all about intention. Sure, there are some people who read people to manipulate them or to influence them underhandedly, but you don't need to be one of them.

Manipulators use people's vulnerabilities and weaknesses against them. They have an acute understanding of people, but they exploit this for their personal gain, and in extreme cases, for their psychotic and sadistic satisfaction.

This book is targeted toward people from the other end of the spectrum from these manipulators. Reading people is understanding the totality of people, weaknesses and vulnerabilities, and also their strengths and potential. It is about using this keen understanding of people in a positive way.

Reading people is not manipulating, but appreciating and honoring. It says to people: "I see, hear, and feel you. I understand." And isn't it human desire to be acknowledged and understood in the right context and with proper intention?

Misconception #4: Reading people is shallow.

It is only in the late 19th century that social sciences such as psychology and sociology started to be considered as academic and scientific endeavors. Even today, there are still people who scoff down on social sciences, considering it inferior to other branches of science such as technology and engineering. Some would even question or undermine the science behind social science.

This notion of inferiority is one of the reasons behind the idea that reading people is a shallow endeavor. In this book, we will explore the science behind reading people to dispel this notion. Specifically, we will tackle some tried and tested ways on how to read people effectively.

On the other hand, there are some who believe that reading people is shallow because it only brushes the surface, and that we can never really fully know a person. While this is true, it doesn't make the endeavor shallow and futile. Understanding people paves deeper connections and fosters more intimate relationships.

Misconception #5: Reading people is mind-reading, magic, and beyond normal.

Lastly, there is this belief that equates people-reading with mind-reading associated with magic shows, new-age stores, and those with extra-sensory perception or ESP. While there are people who can read minds, putting mind-reading on the same pane as people-reading makes the latter seem unachievable unless one has special or magic powers.

However, reading people is not something beyond normal. In fact, it can be achieved by anyone, as long as the person is willing to learn and apply the learning in positive ways.

5 - Types of People-Reader

Now that we have brought into the light and dispelled the common misconceptions on people-reading, let us now examine the common types of people-reader.

On one hand, we have the eccentric people-reader. This is a stereotype promulgated in works of fiction such as Sherlock Holmes from the popular detective series, and Dr. Cal Lightman from the now-defunct crime drama series Lie to Me.

Both are expert people-readers with unconventional ways and volatile personalities. They are respected but feared at the same time. They are the archetypal tricksters or wise-fool. In fiction, they use their people-reading skills to solve problems and cases.

On the other hand, we have the God-like and seemingly all-knowing people-readers. This is a stereotype embodied by fictional characters such as Albus Dumbledore in the Harry Potter series, Ancient One in Doctor Strange, and Professor X in X-Men.

They are all subdued and calm versions of eccentric tricksters. They are the archetypal wise men and women. In fiction, they use their people-reading skills to mentor and empower talented persons.

Lastly, we have the antithesis or the villain versions of the eccentrics and sages. For example, Moriarty versus Sherlock Holmes, Lord Voldemort versus Albus Dumbledore, Dormammu versus Ancient One, Magneto versus Professor X, and Joker versus Batman.

While they are extreme and fictional examples, they are proofs that intention is the differentiating factor between manipulation and empathy. Which type of mind-reader is your peg?

Back to reality, this book is not written to make you a powerful sage, or a famous trickster, or least of all, a supervillain. Rather, it is written to help you become an understanding, kind, and empathic person.

Analyzing and Decoding People

Now that we have examined the why's for reading people, let us know proceed into the how's.

At the heart of understanding human behavior is acknowledging the link between the mind and the body. In general, what a person thinks and feels are reflected in his body and his actions. We can glean this reflection if we just observe closely.

Clenched jaw, balled fists, and teeth grinding show tension and anger. Curled lips and closed eyes characterize a genuine smile. Crossed arms and shrugs may signify resistance. Yawning is a sign of sleepiness, nervousness, and being a normal person and not a psychological case.

The last one may come as a surprise. The explanation is that yawning is a contagious behavior. Maybe you have found yourself yawning involuntarily while reading that last sentence. Guess who are immune to catching the yawning contagion? The answer is psychopaths and sociopaths.

You see, there is merit in studying the anatomy of the human being and how facial expression and body language can tell us more about the person. There is also merit in looking at the movement and preferences of people to decode and analyze them.

How do people carry themselves in social situations, and what do their interactions say about them? How do they write, draw, paint, play sports, cook, and create outputs, and what do their outputs say about them?

Reading people is a valuable skill that we can apply in our personal and professional lives, in our everyday lives and even in critical life-and-death situations.

6 - How Do We Read People Based on Their Facial Expressions?

"There's nothing more interesting

than the landscape of the human face."

—Irvin Kershner, film director

Perhaps you have come across situations wherein you hear or say:

"She has a very expressive face."

"The emotion flashed in his face, so briefly that she almost missed it."

"She smiled and said that she is okay, but her eyes gave her away."

Welcome to the world of facial expressions. As the old adage goes, the eyes are the windows to the soul, and the face says it all.

Facial Expressions in Popular Culture

The study of facial expressions is one of the foundations of the film industry too. Actors and actresses must have vivid facial expressions. In theater, body language is often exaggerated to make the move and the acting visible even to the general admission seats. By contrast, movies and shows made for the television zoom in on the face, and it requires more realistic and subtle acting.

Years before, mimes such as Mr. Bean were popular. They speak with their face, and they exaggerate their facial contortions, resulting to a comic effect.

Nowadays, acting is veered toward more precise facial expressions. Actors and actresses portray emotions accurately so that the viewers can relate well. With realistic portrayals, the lines between fiction and non-fiction are blurred and viewers really get into the show that they cry and laugh and hold their breaths with the characters as if they are part of the show.

Two Types of Facial Expressions

Real life, however, is more complex. Unlike movies with plots and scripts, our lives are more free-flowing and spontaneous, and we don't know what will happen next. Hence, emotions are not as clear-cut.

People sometimes suppress or consciously hide their emotions. Sometimes, people are not even aware that they
repress or unconsciously hide their emotions. But did you
know that even when they hide their emotions, those emotions still leak into their faces, sometimes even for a milli-
second?

Psychologist Dr. Paul Ekman calls these as micro-expressions. These are facial expressions that may flash on the
face for just 1/25 milliseconds. They are fleeting but expose
what the person is truly feeling.

On the other hand, we have macro-expressions. These occur
when we feel single emotions and we don't feel the need to
hide it. This typically happens when we are alone, or with
people we trust and with whom we are comfortable with or
those with whose presence we can let our hair down. These
types of facial expressions last longer than micro-expressions, between half a second to four seconds.

Another key difference between the two types of facial expressions is the wholeness of the expression. For example,
when a person is sad in front of an esteemed friend, she will
show the full expression of sadness, that is, lower corners of

her mouth, raise the inner portion of her eyebrows, and droop her eyelids. She may even cry and confide in her friend what makes her sad.

On the other hand, when that person is sad in public or around people she is not close with, she will try to hide her sadness, but an observant and skilled person will notice a micro-expression of sadness flash across her face in a fraction of a second, perhaps a lowering of the corners of her mouth.

The beauty of facial expressions, whether macro or micro, is that they cannot be hidden, they are universal, and they are analyzable with proper training. For further information, you can check out www.paulekman.com and www.humintell.com, but in this chapter, we will try to cover as such as possible.

While this book is also as descriptive as possible, it may be hard for you to visualize some facial expressions, so feel free to conduct further online research on this topic. Or just look in the mirror, examine your selfies and pictures, search for online photos of different emotions, or watch people to see the depictions of the micro-expressions.

Brief History of Micro-Expressions

The studies on micro-expressions began in 1967, when Dr. Paul, with his colleague Wallace Friesen, started to study deception. They studied clinical cases of patients who claimed that they were not depressed, only to commit suicide afterward.

When Dr. Paul and Wallace replayed the recorded videos of patients in slow motion, they saw micro-expressions that revealed some strong negative emotions despite the efforts of the patients to hide their feelings.

Nowadays, interpreting and reading micro-expressions are useful not just in clinical psychology field, but also in military and negotiation, law enforcement and criminal investigation, sales and marketing, education and counseling, medical intervention, anthropology and consumer research, gaming and deception, popular culture such as movies as discussed earlier, and many other fields.

7 - Facial Expressions of the Seven Universal Emotions

What exactly do we look for when we study facial expressions to determine if people mean what they say or imply? We look for patterns of expressions of emotions.

There are seven universal emotions, as identified by Dr. Paul and Wallace. These are happiness or joy, sadness, surprise, fear, disgust, anger, and contempt. Each emotion is expressed by different facial muscles. Let us examine each one by one.

Happiness or Joy

When a person is happy, they smile. But how do we know if the smile is genuine or forced? When a person smiles, the corners of the mouth rise diagonally. If biologically present, a dimple may appear. The teeth may or may not show. This applies whether the smile is real or staged.

We can detect a genuine smile when it radiates throughout the entire face. The muscles around the eyes are tightened and the cheeks rise up, resulting in wrinkles in the outside end corners of the eyes that we call as Crow's feet. The eyes may twinkle.

The upper set of teeth usually shows as well. The lower set of teeth is not usually shown in a genuine smile. We tend to associate bearing of the lower teeth with a dog's smile or grin.

A genuine laughter also features these facial movements. When a person laughs hard, he or she may even cover his or her mouth. The cheeks or face or neck may blush.

Sadness

We can detect sadness when the corners of the mouth are lowered, sometimes even just slightly, when the inner corners of the eyebrows rise up slightly making the outer corners drop slightly when the upper eyelids droop, and when the eyes lose focus.

Surprise

When a person is surprised, the eyelids pull up causing the eyes to widen and exposing more of its white surface, the entire eyebrows rise or arch up, and sometimes the mouth hangs opens or the jaw drops.

Fear

Fear can be detected with eyebrows raised and pulled together, upper eyelids pulled up, opening the eyes and exposing more of the top white surface. Lower eyelids get tensed and the lips get stretched horizontally, opening the mouth slightly and sometimes exposing the lower teeth.

Disgust

When a person is disgusted, the nose bridge wrinkles, pulling down the eyebrows and raising the cheeks, and the upper lip rises, loosening the lips. The tongue may slightly stick out as if the person wants to vomit.

Anger

We can detect anger when the eyebrows are lowered down and pushed together, causing wrinkles between the eyes. The upper and lower lids push up to the lowered brows. The eyes bulge and glare. The lips are narrowed, tightened, and pressed firmly. The jaw may also clench, and the upper set of teeth may grind with the lower set.

Contempt

Contempt is the newest addition to the list of seven universal emotions. It was added by Dr. Paul in the 1990s, and until now, there are still some debates and discussions on whether it is universal or not.

This is partly because contempt is not a singular emotion, but a combination of different emotions, specifically anger and disgust. We can detect contempt when the lip tightens and rises on one side only. The head may tilt slightly back. The eyes are often neutral. It is like sneering mildly.

Of all the universal emotions, contempt is the only one with asymmetrical manifestation on the face. This lop-lopsidedness is symptomatic of the feeling of being superior over another person, of not being equal or at par with that person.

Note though that there are people who smile on one side only. This doesn't mean that they are in perpetual contempt. Maybe that's really just the way they smile. So it pays to analyze facial expressions alongside personal traits and context.

In general, though, did you know that this micro-expression

is an indicator of divorce and separation?

Relationship psychologist Dr. John Gottman studied thousands of hours of videotaped material showing couples interacting in a laboratory setup which they aptly called Love Lab. Dr. John identified four red flags in a relationship: defensiveness, stonewalling or silent treatment, criticism, and contempt.

Furthermore, throughout the four decades of his research starting in the 1980s, Dr. John found out that contempt is the number predictor of separation.

This means that he can determine with more than 90% accuracy that a couple will separate by just watching them speak with each other, and seeing micro-expressions of contempt along with other negative emotions popping up during the couple's conversation.

Other Emotions

There are other emotions such as anxiety, amusement, bitterness, contentment, courage, doubt, embarrassment, envy, excitement, guilt, helplessness, irritation, jealousy, love, pride, relief, satisfaction, sensory pleasure, shame, shyness, uncertainty, and worry.

Some are combinations of emotions, like contempt. Some are akin to the universal emotions but of different intensity. For instance, amusement is a milder version of happiness, while love is a higher form. Meanwhile, the worry is a milder version of fear, while anxiety is a more intense form.

There are also other feelings that can be detected in the face.

For instance, dilated pupils can be a sign of attraction and readiness for love, although it can also be a medical condition. Pleasure, such as pleasure from eating delicious food, can be signaled by eyes narrowing and even closing, head tilting back, upper back arching back, and making throaty "mmm" sound.

Another example is the eye roll, which signifies annoyance, irritation, or exasperation. Like shaking of the head, eye roll can also mean disbelief, disappointment, or disapproval. Rolling of the eyes is typically associated with sarcasm and contempt, and it is quite an insulting gesture that shows a feeling of superiority.

Another example is lip pursing in a straight line. In the realm of interrogation and confessions, people purse their lips when they are caught lying, so they are "telling it all" or confessing, but at the same time withholding other information, as signaled by their tightly closed lips. It can also signal utter resistance to divulge information. As the idiom goes, "my lips are sealed."

Another popular gesture is shrugging, or when a person purses lips with the sides pushing the cheeks up as if the person is smiling with mouth closed. The eyes also widen and the eyebrows lift as if surprised.

The head tilts to the side. These facial movements are accompanied with body gestures of shoulders shrugging up and with palms pointing up the ceiling. This can mean "I don't know" or "I don't care" or "Well, it's just like that". It can also signal gloating or pride in accomplishments.

Meanwhile, there are some emotions that can totally be concealed in the face, such as embarrassment, envy, and shame. These other emotions can be detected in body language and context.

8 - Deconstructing Facial Expressions

Sometimes, we would come across facial expressions in the course of our everyday conversations, and it is up to us to deduce the emotions and rationale behind the movements of facial muscles.

For example, when talking casually with a colleague at work, you saw him raise his eyebrows. From what we know, brows raised when a person is either surprised or afraid, or other variations of these emotions such as worry. What could possibly have made him surprised, afraid, or worried?

What was the topic when your colleague raised his brows? Did something happen when he raised his brows, for instance, did someone pass by or did he see something in the surrounding that made him raise his brows?

Another example is blushing and paling. There are people who blush visibly, especially in certain cultures. Some are also naturally pale, whether a function of race or medical conditions such as anemia.

In general, taking away racial as well as medical conditions, when people blush, their face takes on a darker or redder color because of the blood that circulates in the face. Some blush just on the cheeks, some up to the ears. They themselves can feel the heat in their face as blood rushes up. This usually signals emotions such as embarrassment or anger.

In cartoons and animations, anger is portrayed as redness going up from the neck, spreading around the face, and reaching the ears, sometimes releasing steam in the ears. This comical representation may be exaggerated, but for anyone who has felt extreme anger, it actually feels like that.

On the other hand, when people's faces turn pale, they can feel the blood draining from their face. This signals fright or shock. Hence, horror and suspense movies are full of pale-faced characters. In real life, we ask someone with a pale face if they are alright because it seems like they have seen a ghost.

It must be noted that blushing also happens when exposed to extreme heat and/or strenuous physical activity such as exercise.

For example, people blush when they are under sun exposure, like staying in the beach or leisurely walking under the sun. This is natural. In fact, this type of blush is a sign of health that the make-up industry tries to replicate with blush-on.

Another example is lifting weights, which can make a person huff and puff, and turn red in the face from all the effort and energy that they exert. It's as if they are angry, but they are just tensed and focused.

Like in other things, when reading changes in the color and intensity of the skin of the facial region, we should look into personal and situational context to understand the meanings and underlying reasons for such changes.

9 - Eye-Gazing and Eye-Reading

Looking a person eye to eye is like peering into their soul. It establishes an emotional connection between persons.

Aside from this, it can also reveal a lot about a person's personality and current emotional and relational state: how the person holds your gaze, how long the person holds your gaze, where the person looks, how the pupils of the eyes dilate or contract, and how fast and how often the person blinks or winks.

However, it must be noted that dilation can also be caused by other factors such as medical condition like mydriasis and substances like alcohol and drugs. Hence, it pays to infer or watch out for the presence of these contributing factors when reading a person through his or her eyes.

A person with dilated pupils may either be attracted to you or perhaps is just drunk or high in cocaine. Be cognizant of context clues and other non-verbal signals.

With the caveat and exceptions out of the way, let us now look at how to read normal eyes, unaffected by these other factors, starting with pupil dilation and contraction.

Pupil Dilation and Contraction

The iris and the pupil dilate and contract to control and adjust the light taken in by the eyes. The pupils are the black center of the eyes, and they are surrounded by a membrane called iris.

When the iris dilates, the pupil widens and opens. This allows the eyes to take in more amount of light as a response to dim or insufficient lighting. Meanwhile, when the iris contracts, the pupil narrows or closes. This restricts the amount of light that enters the eyes as a response to bright light. This is the process of sight.

However, in 1975, Psychologist Eckhard Hess discovered and reported that light is not the only factor that affects dilation, but also interest and arousal.

So when you are talking to a person, and you see the pupils dilate upon looking at the person's eyes, it could mean that the room dimmed, the person found the topic interesting, or perhaps the person is attracted to you.

Looking at the pupils can also serve as a conversation guide. When you reach the point in the conversation when the eyes of the person contracts, it might be a sign to dim the lights, to move to a less bright room, or maybe just change the topic, or go on your way and just save the conversation for later.

That said, be careful not to overdo looking at a person's eyes. This leads us to the next sub-topic.

Eye Contact

How long should you hold a person's gaze? Just long enough to make the person feel interested and noticed, but not uncomfortable or threatened.

Based on a 2015 study done by experimental psychologist Alan Johnston, eye contact with an acquaintance is acceptable for an average of 3.2 seconds, longer if trust and rapport have been established already and also longer if we are listening more than if we are the one talking.

When in an engaging conversation, a person focuses on the other person's face 80% of the time but look at the eyes for a few seconds only, then looks at the other parts of the face such as between the eyes, the nose, or the lips. Expert executive interviewers suggest looking at the point between the eyes or the top of the nose to avoid eye contact fatigue.

Note however that there are also persons that veer away from eye contact, and it can be a cultural thing or a personal preference. In general, though, we can detect lying and deception when a person evades and avoids gaze, or when the person gazes too long and/or too intense and still and unblinking, or what we call as overly persistent eye contact.

Deception can also be indicated by the quality of eye contact when responding. A person typically breaks eye contact to think or to consider some points that come up during the conversation, then looks in the eyes again to respond or answer.

But when a person wants to hide something, the person looks away even when answering. Or the person may look straight in the eyes, then compensate with other non-verbal afterward, such as rubbing nose, heaving a sigh, rubbing the eyes, or rolling the eyes.

Eye Direction and Focus of the Gaze

Where does the person look? In between eye connects, in which direction does the person look when thinking? Looking to the left generally indicates recalling memories, remembering facts, and reminiscing events.

Meanwhile, looking to the right typically indicates more creative thought processes. This may be an indicator of lying and deception as the person may be a creating another version of events in his/her mind.

Just a caveat though that this may be reversed if the person is left-handed. So look for patterns of behavior instead of just relying on one indicator.

The focus of the gaze is also a way to determine what the person values or holds important. Hence, photos and videos are good indicators of a person's values systems and precious moments, persons, and things.

Another way to determine what a person considers precious is to look at where the person looks when laughing in a group. The tendency is to seek out affirmation and share positive moments with the person closest to our hearts.

Blinking, Winking, Crying, and Other Eye Movements

A normal person blinks for about 6 to 10 times in 1 minute. However, our emotions can change this blink rate. For instance, when we are in a state of arousal or following a period of surprise and excitement, we tend to blink faster and more often. This might make pupil dilation more difficult to spot for amateur eye readers.

Blinking fast and winking are indications of flirting too, and some cultures especially Eastern or Asian culture may consider these gestures too straightforward and even offensive.

Another eye gesture that expresses emotions is crying. People cry when they are sad or grieving, and also when they are extremely happy. Some people can cry at will, such as actors and actresses. When crying is forced for the sake of deception and manipulation, it is called crocodile tears, termed after crocodiles who shed tears while eating their prey.

Applications and Limitations of Reading Facial Expressions

The truth can really be gleaned from the face. We can tell a lot about the current emotional state of a person if we just take time to look at his/her face. Just a caveat, though, that staring at people can make people feel uncomfortable. Some also consider it rude. So do it discreetly and tactfully. Besides, macro-expressions and micro-expressions take just seconds to flash in the face.

Knowing about facial expressions also enable you to be mindful of how the muscles of your face move. The facial muscles of a normal person without any medical condition are voluntary muscles. This means they don't move on their own accord. This means we, or at least our mind and body, can control the facial muscles. But sometimes, our subconscious brain knows better.

We feel something negative but don't really know what it is, but a trained or observant person may see a micro-expression of anger. If we are in touch with our inner selves and our feelings, we need not be oblivious and we wouldn't need a stranger to analyze our feelings for us.

A facial analysis may not always work. For instance, it is not relevant for those who have undergone Botox and other procedures that prohibit movement of facial muscles, as well as those who have encountered accidents or have genetic disorders that limit movement of facial muscles.

But these are exceptions. In general, universal emotions are called such because they apply to a wide range of people and situations.

Practice analyzing people by watching their facial expressions. Start with the people you deal with every day. Look more closely at their faces, and perhaps you may be surprised with the emotions flashing across their faces that you might have missed otherwise.

10 - How Do We Read People Based on Their Body Language?

"A body talks."

—Anne Parillau, French actress

Sometimes, people say one thing but mean the other. Such mismatch between words and actions has inspired essays, novels, poems, and even songs. Perhaps we can relate to Justin Bieber's love song that goes: "What do you mean? When you nod your head yes, but you want to say no."

It's not just in personal relationships. Sometimes we encounter dissonance in the workplace too, and even in our encounters with strangers.

We can spot mismatch by examining verbal language vis-à-vis body language. In the end, the body doesn't lie.

By themselves, body language is ambiguous and varies from person to person. Reality is less definitive and clear-cut than the detective and crime-solving shows we see on television. However, it is worth noting some commonalities and generalizations about body language.

Why is this important and necessary?

Nick Morgan, a communications coach, said that reading body language is not really a matter of reading people's thoughts and mental processes, but more on grasping the emotional intent behind their actions.

Humans function both on the conscious and unconscious levels. Sometimes, we filter our words and try to mask our feelings by doing the quintessential poker face, but unbeknownst to us, our emotions have already been displayed briefly in our bodies long before our conscious minds have finished the attempt to mask.

Learning about body language can help us spot and detect these subconscious actions, as well as try to understand the emotional root or intent behind them.

This chapter tells some of the common gestures and their possible meanings, specifically the mental and emotional states which prompted the subconscious physical manifestations.

How They Shake Hands Is How They Prefer to Learn

The way people shake hands tells a lot about their personality. Specifically, it offers an insight into their learning style. The VAK model of learning style states that a person interacts, learns about, and navigates the world in one of the following ways: visual, auditory, and kinesthetic.

There are plenty of tests to determine a person's learning style, but body language is the easiest way to do so. How? Just shake hands.

Does the person look at you eye to eye as you shake hands as if the person wants to look deep into your eyes and peer into your heart, mind, and spirit? Chances are, this person is a visual person.

Does the person tilt one side of the head and ear toward you, as if the person wants to hear you and your words better? This person may be an auditory person. Their handshakes may tend to be limp.

Sometimes, people consider limp handshakes as a sign of being timid or being non-committal. However, it can just be because the person is auditory and always shakes hands like that because they focus their energy more on their sense of hearing more than the sense of touching. Knowing this can help us correct or temper our assumptions and initial impressions of people.

Does the person grip your hands very firmly, or use two hands to shake your hand? Does the person go in for a hug, whether partial or full? Does the person pat your shoulder with the other hand, or wrap the arms around your shoulders? Most likely, this person is a kinesthetic person.

There are many applications of knowing this classification.

When it comes to education, a visual person learns best by illustrations and drawings, auditory by listening intently to words, and kinesthetic by demonstrations and movement. A good teacher understands that students have different needs, and prepares curriculum and classroom materials that engage all learning styles.

This can also be applied in the corporate and business world, where shaking hands is the common way of introduction. For instance, a salesperson can tailor-fit the sales pitch on the VAK style of the potential client.

In the same way as the teacher, a good salesperson prepares materials and spiels for all learning styles, then deduces the learning style of the client when they shake hands, uses this information to sell better, adjusting along the way based on verbal and non-verbal feedback from the client.

Communication requires attentive and responsive focus. This goes for sales as well as in friendships. This leads us to the next application of VAK style.

How They Express Love Is How They Prefer to Be Loved

How does your loved ones, special someone, and close ac-quaintances prefer to be loved? Sometimes, we shower people with tender loving care, for instance by giving gifts or doing things for them. But they don't seem to feel it, and they might even accuse us of not loving them. Or it might be vice versa, wherein we don't feel loved even if people say they do love us in their own ways.

In any case, this frustrates both parties, and the relationship is affected when the parties speak different love languages. In 1995, author Gary Chapman wrote about the five love languages: gifts, quality time, words of affirmation, acts of service, and physical touch.

Again, there are tests to determine this. But there are two easy ways to determine.

First, via VAK learning style, when we meet someone for the first time, whether as a platonic or romantic prospect, we shake their hands. And this can be a good gauge of their love language.

Visual persons might prefer gifts and physical presence, whether in the form of quality time, acts of service, and physical touch. Auditory persons want words of affirmation. Kinesthetic persons need actions and touch, and similar with visual persons, this can be in the form of quality time, acts of service, and physical touch.

Sometimes, VAK and love language vary due to cultural and familial upbringing. For instance, a visual person might clamor for words of affirmation more than gifts because it was something lacking while the person was growing up. The point is, while VAK is a good way to initially read a per-son's love language, it might not be accurate, and we need to revise our knowledge as we go along.

This leads us to the second of the two easy ways to determine love language. We just need to study how the person expresses love. You see, how we love is how we want to be loved. Once you understand and accept this, you love people better and you save yourself from heartbreak and frustrations.

How They Walk into a Room Signal Confidence and Power

Posture projects confidence and commands respect. Have you ever seen someone walk into a room, and instantly come to the conclusion that they lack confidence or perhaps is just an assistant, a junior, or a newbie? Have you ever seen someone walk into a room, and instantaneously know that they are the boss or the one in charge?

What is it about them that made you think so? It is about body language, specifically posture and stance, and how they occupy space and move around the space around them.

A person who lacks confidence would most probably enter the room tentatively and shyly, with slouched shoulders and head bowed, looking down at the floor, perhaps with their hands in their pockets. It's as if they don't want to be in the room in the first place, as if they want the walls or the floor to swallow them, or as if they just want to hide or be invisible. Their focus is more inward.

On the other hand, a confident person may stride into the room with erect posture and eyes scanning the room, acknowledging the presence of other people, perhaps even smiling or nodding at each person nearby.

They seem to fill the space around them, and their gestures are more expansive. Their focus is more outward. They exude power, command respect, and inspire engagement with the people in the room.

Powerful people also feel more comfortable touching people such as tapping the shoulder or the upper arm to get someone's attention, to greet someone, to show appreciation for someone, or to stress a point during conversations and discussions.

Less confident and less powerful persons may feel awkward to do so. However, individual and cultural sensibilities apply to this. For example, some Asian cultures may be less touchy even in personal relationships, as opposed to some

Western cultures wherein platonic and wholesome touchiness may be deemed appropriate even for business and professional setting.

It can also be the way they dress up. Do they "power dress" and are their clothes neat and well-pressed, shoes on-point and well-polished? Are they well-groomed from head to toe? Are they over-the-top, just-right, understated, sloppy, or untidy?

How They Open and Close Their Limbs Signal Openness and Resistance

The crossing of the arms and legs is a universal sign of resistance, especially in the realm of negotiations. Note though that there are exceptions to the rule. Perhaps the weather is cold and the person is crossing arms to keep the cold away.

Maybe the person always crosses legs as a force of habit. Perhaps the person just wants to get comfortable and laid back, and crossing arms and legs is the way to do this. Again, reading people must always have context.

Having said this caveat, the general rule of thumb is that physically closing the body, like when crossing the arms and legs, indicate psychological closing or mental and/or emotional resistance to ideas and options. It may also come with a host of emotions such as anger, arrogance, or contempt.

When in negotiations and one of the stakeholders sits back and crosses arms and legs, this is a signal for the person talking to change tactics to maneuver around the apparent display of resistance to the ideas presented.

Conversely, physically opening the body, like when opening the arms and legs, signals internal openness.

For example, think about when a person opens the arms into a hug or one of the universal signs of attraction that we always see in movies. Another example is when a guy extends and puts his arms in the back of the chair where a female is seated.

If the girl doesn't flinch, the guy may eventually put his arms around the shoulder. If the girl still doesn't flinch, the guy may even go in for a kiss, if they are already at that stage of their relationship.

How They Mirror Your Actions Signify Connection

Do you have a close friend with whom you have a special bond with? Perhaps you finish each other's sentences. You speak without words. For females, you may even find your monthly period coming at the same time each month. It seems our bodies and spirits sync when we are close with someone.

This level of connection is akin to mirroring. For instance, you just met someone you like. You may find yourself mirroring their gestures and even how they say certain words and phrases.

It can be conscious or subconscious. This trick can also be used in negotiations. In any case, mirroring the actions of the other person shows that you are paying attention to them and that you are receptive to their presence and actions.

So whenever you come across a person who mirrors your moves, tilting head or moving hands the same way as you, it's either the person likes you a lot or is trying to manipulate you. Gauge their intention based on the context. Are they subconsciously mirroring you?

Can they look you in the eye with sincerity? Or do you feel that they are consciously mimicking you as if they are almost mocking you? Why do you think they want to establish a connection? Is it because they want or need something from you? Or do they seriously and genuinely just want to get to know you more or bond with you?

How They Nod or Shake Their Heads Indicate Emotions Beyond Approval and Rejection

Nodding means yes while shaking head means no. In real life, things are not as simple as that.

Exaggerated or profuse nodding can mean that the person seeks approval because the person is worried about what you think of them, or anxious that you doubt their ability to do a task or follow your instruction to them.

This can work against them as we might perceive those who nod profusely as insincere, needy, or weak. To project a powerful and confident image, nod only when necessary and when you mean it, and avoid over-nodding.

That said, nodding continuously while smiling indicates being pleased or being pleasantly surprised with a person, a happening, or an idea, for example when you experience or witness a eureka moment.

In more casual settings, nodding can function as a form of greeting or acknowledgment of an acquaintance's presence, usually accompanied with a slight raising of the eyebrows and a smile.

On the other side of the coin, exaggerated or profuse shaking can mean intense rejection bordering on disgust and even contempt, or panic when accompanied with an afraid look.

Meanwhile, slow and continuous shaking of the head can indicate disappointment when accompanied with an angry frown or contempt, or signal warning or caution when accompanied with a look of fear. It can also mean being caught off guard in a positive way by an unbelievable event or circumstance. Think of slow claps accompanied by slow shaking of the head.

How the Muscles of the Bodies Tense Signal Discomfort, Anxiety, and Stress

Stress manifests in the body in the form of tightened muscles such as jaw clenching, shoulders hiking up to the ears, eyebrows furrowing, and fidgeting. These are all responses of the body to stressors.

When talking about stress, we might think of chronic stress. However, it is also worthwhile to look at the everyday stresses that we might encounter, especially since chronic stress starts from these small stresses that escalate and endure.

For instance, when talking with a person, you might notice any of these body languages signaling stress. What were you talking about that might have caused such stress response? How do you shift the conversation to move them from a place of discomfort to assurance?

Or perhaps the stressor came from outside the conversation. What occurred in the environment that put stress on them? Is there anything you can do or are you in a position to help them?

How the Crowning Glory Tells a Story about Rainy Days, Mondays, and Bad Hair Days

"Bad hair day" is an idiom used by people to describe days that are less than ideal. For instance, when unfortunate events occur one after the other, causing people to feel sad and down, which some people associate with rainy days. Or when things don't go as planned, or when good things end and dreaded things happen, making people feel lethargic and moody, which some people associate with Mondays.

Sometimes though, bad hair days happen literally. In cases like this, we can take cues from the state of the hair of a person.

For instance, your office mate who usually keeps her hair tidy and well-kept in a ponytail or bun arrives in the office with her hair all over the place, and stress all over her face. You sense something is amiss, and ask her if she is alright or how she is doing.

Or for example, your friend who usually keeps his hair ruffled even when going out suddenly arrives at a party with his hair combed neatly and he even applied hair gel. You teasingly ask him who he is eyeing in the party.

In general, regardless of hair type, color, cut, and amount, the hair is a good indicator of how put-together a person is, how in-control the person is about his/her day, how self-aware the person is what fits him/her, and how much the person cares for social conventions. It tells about the personality, temperament, and current mood or state of the person.

It's not just the hair, actually. We can take cues on the grooming, make-up, attire, and overall appearance of the person. And again, take cues from both the person's get-up and the context.

For instance, when in weddings and formal gatherings wherein attendees are typically required to dress up, there is no need to second-guess people for dressing up. Unless if the person is known not to dress up even in such events or unless the person dresses over-the-top or the other way around.

By studying a person's overall appearance from head to toe, and comparing this with their usual appearance and mind-ing also the context of the situation, we can gain insight into who the person is and what they are feeling at the moment.

These observations can serve as a springboard to reaching out to people with care and empathy, such as when we ask if the person is okay or how is the day going.

Furthermore, keen observations can be brave conversation-starters too. For instance, "Hello! I noticed how your dress stands out in the crowd. I love that it's avaunt-garde! Where is the dress from?" Or perhaps, "Nice hair color! It suits you! Curiously, what made you decide on this color?" Then their responses can confirm, add on, or debunk your initial hypotheses about their personalities.

How the Position of the Chin and the Neck Indicates Level of Confidence from Lacking to Arrogance

A confident and poised person typically maintains a straight neck and chin level with the ground, looking in front and neither up nor down.

A chin that juts out pushes the face up, which makes the

eyes appear to look down on people, and this signals arrogance or stubbornness.

Meanwhile, a chin that curls toward the neck cause the head to bow down, and a person who maintains this posture all the time can be construed as shy or lacking in confidence.

How They Sit and Stand Indicate Posture and Confidence

We often hear from our elders and from other people: "Sit up straight!" or "Stand up straight!" Their advice is meant to remind us of the value of keeping proper posture to prevent back and spine issues.

Slouching and overarching of the back may be permissible occasionally to stretch and move the back muscles, but maintaining these poses for extended and repeated periods of time can lead to a host of health problems.

Beyond medical issues and proper posture, standing and sitting with a straight spine can indicate being raised properly, being comfortable in one's body, being in control of one's emotions and thoughts, and being in charge of a situation.

A person who is chronically slumping or slouching may come across as lacking in self-confidence, someone who does not feel good or not comfortable with himself or herself. However, when you see a person with generally good posture slumping, whether slightly or fully, this can be an indicator that the person needs some help in that particular moment.

Whereas straight backs signal control and command respect, slouching appeals to the sympathy of people. Too straight of a back may make one look like a military-like strict and unbending person, while too slouched back may make people feel sorry for you.

It is not just the back that we need to look at, but also the position of the limbs, especially the legs. If the legs are crossed, is there a reason for the person to feel resistant about or perhaps this is just how they always sit? If the legs are down and crossed at the ankles, it is a sign of good posture.

If the legs are splaying out, the person seems to be too relaxed and too lax, and it may also signal being sloppy and inconsiderate. If you take the public transportation, perhaps you can remember a time when you were irritated or annoyed because a person is sitting too wide-legged, invading the personal spaces of other people.

Aside from the position of the legs, are the legs shaking or are the feet tapping? Like fidgeting the hands, leg-shaking and foot-tapping may signal anxiety, stress, irritation, or impatience. Note however that some people always do these habitually, oftentimes irking or distracting the people around them.

Deliberately tapping a foot or tapping the fingers definitely signal impatience, telling people to move faster, but these non-verbal cues are sometimes deemed passive-aggressive or rude and may be ignored by people.

How People Gesticulate or Move Their Hands Signal Control and Calmness

Perhaps you know of a person who gestures and moves hands a lot, or a person who fidgets a lot and who cannot seem to sit in one place. Perhaps you have been in a presentation wherein the presenter waves and gestures hands all over the place while speaking in a high-pitched voice.

Gestures indicate emotions, and over-gesticulating can reveal to the world a barrage of uncontrolled emotions. It signals lack of self-control and even lack of self-awareness.

A good presenter uses gestures to make points, and as much as possible avoids unnecessary gestures that may distract the audience from the material being presented verbally and visually.

From the receiving end, a good audience sits still and just rests hands on the lap or on the table, gently holding the hands together, neither clutching nor fidgeting, and not crossing the arms akimbo, as these gestures may distract and send worrying signals and cues to the person talking or presenting, unless of course if the audience intends to send some non-verbal message to the speaker.

How People Breathe Signal Their Inner State

The breathing patterns of people can offer us insight into their inner thoughts and feelings, specifically how fast they are breathing, how deep, how even or rhythmic, and from where is the breath coming from.

Each person has a different way of breathing, and it pays to look at variations from their usual.

Are they breathing quicker and shorter? Maybe they are nervous or anxious.

Are their breaths slower, more rhythmic, and deeper? Maybe they are in a relaxed state and good mood.

Are they breathing more deeply but irregularly? Maybe they are tensed. Or perhaps they are catching their breath after an exhausting activity.

Breathing can also signify health issues such as respiratory and circulatory issues. If someone close to you starts to breathe differently, look at the environment for possible things that could have affected their breathing.

If the change in breathing is more permanent or persisting, then it may be good also to tactfully inquire about the status of their health and even suggest seeing a doctor for preventive measures.

How to Read Body Language More Accurately and More Effectively

In this chapter, we discussed the various gestures and body movements, and their possible meanings. As Nick Morgan reminds us, body language must be analyzed alongside verbal and another non-verbal language.

Moreover, we must take into account people's temperament, personality, cultural upbringing, individual preferences and idiosyncrasies, and situation or context. Furthermore, we must also factor in our own personalities and biases.

What do we observe from people? What do these tell us about people in the here and now? Where are they coming from? Where are we coming from? What factors could possibly cloud our take on the situation and our understanding of people?

This is an active thought process, and it can be quite taxing to do this all the time, in all social interactions, to analyze all non-verbal language that we encounter.

The good news is that we don't have to subject ourselves to

this every single time, every second of the day. We are naturally good at this. At least, our subconscious minds are. We just have to be mindful of our subconscious mental and emotional processing of the world, until it becomes automatic and accurate.

11 - How Do We Read People Based On Their Personality and Temperament?

"Try to understand people. If you understand each other, you will be kind to each other. Knowing a person well never leads to hate, and almost always leads to love."

—John Steinbeck, writer

Personality sums up a person's attitudes, values, memories, relationships, skills, habits, hobbies, temperament, disposition, and other personal characteristics that define the person.

Some people have obvious personality traits. For instance, as you talk to a person, you instantly know that the person is a charismatic extrovert, even after just talking to them for a couple of seconds.

Sometimes, it may not be as apparent. For example, even after talking to someone for hours, you still cannot spell out their personality type.

Other times, it can be surprising too. For instance, the same person who you labeled as charismatic extrovert confesses that she is actually an introvert, and you were shocked because you didn't detect it.

Sometimes, we can know a person for years, spend every day with them, then they say or do something that shakes us because we didn't see it coming. They suddenly reveal a layer of their personality that we haven't seen before, but may in hindsight be actually right in front of our eyes all along.

People are complex and evolving beings, and as people ourselves and being in the same situation as them, we tend to overlook some aspects or take their idiosyncrasies for granted. Hence, from time to time, it is good to actually take a step back, and just try to examine and understand the layers of the people around us, and hopefully, gain a deeper appreciation of people.

But how do we read people's layers and facets? We will now tackle two major theories or models about personality:

- The Theory of 16 Personalities

- The Theory of 4 Temperaments

12 - Reading People's Personality Traits

Have you come across profiles of people with 4 letters in them, such as ESFJ or INTJ? This is from the Myers-Briggs Type Indicator or MBTI.

Isabel Briggs Myers and her mother Katharine Cook Briggs developed this system to describe how a person interacts with the world, how a person perceives and processes information, how a person deals with emotions, and how a person approaches tasks and makes decisions.

Isabel and Katharine based their classification system from Carl Jung. MBTI type is determined by taking a self-accomplished questionnaire. It is an introspective system.

However, you can do an educated guess on a person's MBTI, provided that you know how the classification system works and that you have dealt with the person for at least a couple of weeks or months, whether personally or professionally.

As we go through this chapter, think about someone close to you and try to identify which traits best describes them. Or you can analyze yourself. Then perhaps, later on, you can take the test or ask your loved ones to take the test online.

The model that we will tackle is a close adaptation of MBTI. Instead of 4 letters, there are 5 letters to this personality classification. This version is devised by Neris Analytics, and you can check out their website, www.16personalities.-com. Feel free to compare and contrast with the official MBTI from the website www.myersbriggs.org.

The beauty about the 16 Personalities proposed by Neris Analytics is that they present the results in a spectrum. For example, instead of just saying that you are an INTJ, it tells you that you are 80% introvert, 70% intuitive, 60% thinking, and 51% judging. Hence, you will not panic or be surprised if you turn into INTP when you take the test after some years.

Moreover, the Neris model gives another letter, an auxiliary classification, to describe confidence and response to stress, whether a person is assertive or turbulent.

Overall, it is more fluid and more mindful of the complexity, fluidity, and intricacies of personality. Let us now go through the 5 aspects one by one.

I or E: Introvert or Extrovert

Introversion is one of the most misunderstood psychological traits. The common knowledge is that introverts are shy and timid, while extroverts are outgoing and people-person. While this thinking may have some basis, it is inaccurate to equate introversion with shyness and timidity, extroversion with confidence and social skills.

The good thing is that people are becoming more educated on what introverts and extroverts really are, thanks to the availability of information in schools and online, as well as in books that shed light on these psychological traits such as the bestselling books "Quiet: The Power of Introverts in a World That Can't Stop Talking Kindle Edition" by Susan Cain and "The Genius of Opposites: How Introverts and Extroverts Achieve Extraordinary Results Together" by Jennifer B. Kahnweiler PhD.

You can read more on these resources for a more in-depth understanding of this aspect of personality. However, worry not, because we will discuss the main points in this chapter.

Going back to our example, the question to ask is: what is it about introversion that may make some introverts appear shy and timid, and what is it about extroversion that may make some extroverts appear outgoing and confident?

From a psychological lens, introversion-extroversion is a spectrum that describes how a person interacts with the world.

There are many ways to identify an introvert versus an extrovert, but there are 2 main ways to distinguish one from the other.

First, how does social interaction make them feel, and what effect does this have on their preference for activities and hobbies? Introverts find social interaction exhausting and taxing, and hence they seek more solitary activities. Meanwhile, extroverts find social interaction energizing and invigorating, and hence they thrive in group activities.

Another way of putting this is, do they prefer their inner world or the outer world? Do they prefer to live in their heads or to engage with the world?

Second, how do they respond to external stimulation such as things they hear, smell, or see? Introverts are sensitive to these things because they get agitated easily. Meanwhile, extroverts have a higher threshold for stimulation, and instead of being agitated, they turn enthusiastic and excited when stimulated.

As babies, introverts typically cry a lot, because even the slightest sound can affect them. Meanwhile, extroverts are typically quiet and smiling babies.

These two facets serve as the rationale behind the stereotype that introverts prefer coffee shops and libraries or just staying at home, while extroverts prefer bars and party places or going out in general.

It must be noted that these descriptions compare the extreme ends of the spectrum. However, since introversion-extroversion is a continuum, introverts may display some extroverted behavior and vice versa.

Moreover, belongingness and community are psychological needs based on Abraham Maslow's Hierarchy of Needs, and even the most introverted person may get that urge to socialize every once in a while. On the other hand, rest is a basic physiological need, and even the most extroverted person would definitely need to take a break from the world every once in a while.

Furthermore, ambiverts do exist. They are those who fall in

the middle of the spectrum. They may be 55% extrovert and 45% introvert, or vice versa. They toe the line between introversion and extroversion.

With these descriptions of the traits, are you an introvert, an extrovert, or an ambivert? Then think of the people that you have in your life. Are they introverts, extroverts, or ambiverts?

S or N: Sensing or Intuitive

The second aspect is about how people perceive the world and process information.

Sensing people rely on their senses to do this. They observe physical reality, such as what they see, hear, smell, touch, and taste. They pay attention to facts and details, either present or past, before coming to conclusions or looking at the big picture. They are down-to-earth, experiential, and practical. Their preference for pragmaticism and stability is apparent in their strong and persistent habits.

On the other hand, intuitive people rely on their intuition and imagination. They look for meanings and patterns. They read between the lines, looking at hidden meanings, and seeing the big picture first before looking at the nitty-gritty.

They rely on mental models, abstract theories, and impressions rather than facts and hands-on experience. They are curious and open-minded. They think beyond past and present and look for future possibilities. Novelty appeals to them.

Similar with introversion-extroversion, sensing-intuitive aspect also falls in a spectrum. To read people, it pays to look at how they generally act across different aspects of their lives, both personally and professionally. How do they remember events? How do they analyze a situation? How do they solve problems? These are the facets that you need to look for.

Knowing this is critical to help you deal with persons. Whether your spouse, kid, team member, superior or clients are sensing or intuitive, you need to adjust your spiels to appeal to how they process information. This would make it easier for them to break things down and act or react accordingly.

For example, if your boss is more on the sensing side, you may want to present your case or problem going from micro to macro or from facts to the big picture. On the other hand, if your boss is intuitive, state the macro or big picture first, before laying out the micro details.

In the end, ask yourself: Are you more sensing, more intuitive or somewhere in between? How about the people close to you?

T or F: Thinking or Feeling

The third aspect is how people make decisions and cope with emotions.

Similar with introversion and extroversion, this aspect is also quite misunderstood. A feeling is often confused with emotions, while thinking is taken as intelligence.

However, everyone has emotions and everyone is capable of intellectualizing. In fact, we use thinking to decide on some aspects of life, feeling for other decisions. We oftentimes base it on what the situation calls for. Sometimes, we use them in conjunction, considering both the hard and soft aspects of a scenario.

So what is this aspect about?

It is not about situational decision-making preference, but about general preference on how to make decisions. In general, across different aspects of life and various situations, does a person prefer to put more weight on the hard aspects such as logic, facts, and principles? Or does a person prefer to put more weight on the soft aspects such as compassion and concern?

Does a person like to tackle an issue headlong, or prefer instead to skirt around the issue? The former characterizes a thinking personality, the latter a feeling personality.

Thinking persons tend to be rational and objective when making decisions. They prefer to use logic over emotions, efficiency over harmony and cooperation, truth over tact, a task over people. They think about the pros and cons of a situation and do not let biases and personal matters cloud their logic and principles. They strive to be fair but may come across as cold, indifferent, or uncaring.

On the other hand, feeling persons tend to be emotional and sensitive when making decisions. They focus on emotions, harmony and cooperation, tactfulness, and values. They are people-oriented. They consider the perspectives of other people, and they think about the possible effects of decisions on people. They strive to be empathic but may come across as too warm or too soft, sentimental, or overcautious.

Of the two, which seems more natural or effortless for you? Which side of the spectrum are each people close to you comfortable with?

J or P: Judging or Perceiving

The fourth aspect is how people prefer to live their outer lives, whether they are judging or perceiving. Judging is often confused with being judgmental, but these are totally different things. Some equate this aspect also with organization skills.

However, judging-perceiving spectrum is neither about judging people or situations nor having good planning skills. Rather, it reflects people's approach to planning, working, and decision-making.

Since this is about how people live their outer lives, it is about the behaviors and habits that can be seen by other people. Hence, of the various aspects, this can be the most noticeable. It can be quite confusing too because it marries other aspects such as introversion-extroversion, thinking-feeling, and sensing-intuitive. Let's break it down.

Judging persons tend to use their decision-making preference, whether they are thinking or feeling, in their outer lives. They are quite decisive. They put a premium on thoroughness, organization, clarity, structure, planning, and predictability.

People may describe them as orderly and organized. Indeed, they like to plan to keep things under control, and they feel uncomfortable when nothing is definite or decided. They are fans of to-do lists. They prefer to delay gratification, and they believe in working first before playing, and they typically break down tasks to avoid rushing when deadlines loom.

Again, do not confuse judging personality with being judgmental. It must not be taken as close-mindedness also. Judging individuals just want their outer world to have a semblance of order and direction, however, deep inside, they can actually be open and flexible.

On the other end of the spectrum, perceiving people tend to use their information processing preference, whether sensing or intuitive, in their outer lives. Their way of life tends to be spontaneous.

People may describe them as prospecting, flexible, and relaxed. Indeed, they are comfortable with uncertainty, as they like to improvise and adapt to the outside world. They think of work as a mixture of work and play. Deadlines stimulate them. Working in bursts of energy, they often find themselves beating deadlines.

Do not confuse perceiving with having a quick, keen, and accurate perceptions about the outside world. Do not mistake it also as being unorganized, scatter-brained, or indecisive. Perceiving individuals just prefer to keep their options open in the outer world, but deep inside, they can be decisive and organized.

Which one do you associate yourself more? How about the people around you?

A or T: Assertive or Turbulent

The fifth and last aspect is an addition of Neris Analytics to the standard MBTI. It is about how confident people are in their decisions and abilities. It acts as some sort of internal sensor on how we react to external stimuli such as success or failure, feedback, stress or pressure, and unforeseen events.

Assertive persons have self-assurance and even temper and are typically resistant to stress. They are quite relaxed, refusing to worry too much, to push themselves too much or too hard to achieve goals, to beat themselves over past mistakes or shortcomings.

For them, past is past, and what's been done is done. Expectedly, they tend to have higher life satisfaction and more confidence in their abilities to handle challenges.

On the other hand, turbulent persons are self-conscious. Being sensitive to stress, they get emotional in the sense that they experience a wider range of emotions versus assertive persons when stimulated. They tend to be driven toward goals and success, and may be perfectionists and always eager to better themselves. They think a lot about past mistakes, as well as the future or the direction of their lives.

Personality Traits: Putting Them All Together

In the end, you will have 5 letters to describe yourself and the people around you. There are 16 combinations of MBTI, and there are various names to describe each one of them. For instance, INTJ and INTP are called masterminds, while ESFJ is called the provider or the consul. These labels vary by source and literature.

Beyond labels though, it is more important to look at each aspect as a spectrum, and looking at the overarching and holistic traits of each type.

What has this exercise taught you about yourself and about other people? How can you use this classification to understand people more, as well as your interactions with them?

Before we end this subsection, it is necessary to remind that this 5-letter classification consists of spectrums. Hence, classification may vary across life stages. It would also be interesting to find out in which sides of each spectrum are you and the people around you falling into different points in your lives.

This is a timely reminder that people are complex and evolving creatures and that any attempt to understand them must be done with an open and perceiving mind.

14 - How Do We Read People Based on Their Interests?

"Tell me what you pay attention to and I will tell you who you are."

—José Ortega y Gasset, philosopher

When we meet someone for the first time, we often ask them what they like to do for fun, or what activities they like to engage in aside from work and chores. We inquire about their hobbies, interests, and quirks.

Do they like reading? What books do they like to read? What genre? Which authors? What was the last book they read? What are they currently reading? Which book or author will they never ever read? Which book or author do they regret reading if any? Which book can they read over and over again, or bring to an island if they are stranded?

Replace reading and books with movies, music, artwork, mountains, biking trails, fashion and clothes, cars, toys, and other hobbies. This small talk is all about looking for common ground, or a topic from which we can get to know a person more.

Once we find something that we have in common, it is

easier to build rapport and trust. We feel more comfortable with people with whom we share some things in common.

Furthermore, just exploring these facets can already tell us a lot about the people we have just met, about their personalities, preferences, and temperaments, even without asking and telling outright.

For instance, are their interests more home-based, or do they seem like they go out on adventures a lot, or are they somewhere in between? Do they prefer more solitary or social activities? When talking about their hobbies, are they technical or functional, or emotional and passionate? Do they like to consume or create? Do they put a premium on material and physical things, or are they more experiential?

If we are lucky, they can even show us some of their creations or outputs, perhaps a poem or essay they have written, a painting they have drawn, a picture they have sketched, a photo they have taken, a video of them dancing, a picture of them surfing or doing poses on the yoga mat, or perhaps they can sample us with their singing skills.

Or maybe they can show us the mementos and other stuff that have sentimental values for them.

14 - HOW DO WE READ PEOPLE BASED ON THEIR INTERESTS?

When we look at their creations and personal artifacts, we gain further insight into who they are as persons.

This is because when we do something, we project a piece of ourselves in that thing. Hence, things like paintings and blog posts can provide us a glimpse not just into the abilities of people, but also on their internal states, mentally, emotionally, socially, and psychologically.

Are they happy, steady, or troubled? Are they always like this? Then that points to their temperament. Or is it something temporary? Maybe they are undergoing some events in their lives that are leading them to such states that manifest in the things that they do. Do they need space or intervention?

These are the questions that can lead us to a better understanding of people, whether we have just met them for the first time, or whether we have known them for quite some time.

13 - Reading People's Temperaments

Unlike personality which may change across life stages, a person's temperament tends to be more stable across a lifetime. Temperament is a natural predisposition and innate tendencies of a person. It is biological more than learned, nature more than nurture.

Temperament comes from the Latin word "temperamentums" which means mixtures, which is an appropriate term for a persona's blend of mental, emotional, and psychological traits rooted in physiological makeup.

The Temperament Theory has its roots from pre-modern psychology, from ancient philosophers and physiologists who explored how each temperament corresponds to certain bodily fluids and body organs. For instance, sanguine temperament is associated with blood and liver, choleric with yellow bile and spleen, melancholic with black bile and gallbladder, and phlegmatic with phlegm and brain and lungs.

While modern psychology acknowledges the origins of the temperament theory, it tends to veer away from these physiological connections and instead delves into the behavioral traits and characteristics of each temperament.

One of the most comprehensive and concise books written about temperaments is "Personality Plus: How to Understand Others by Understanding Yourself" by Florence Littauer. To know about your temperament, you can take a free online test. You can also ask your family, friends, and colleagues to answer. Your answers and results may surprise you or maybe not.

You can also take a shortcut by reading descriptions of each type, and examine yourself to determine which best describes you and the people around you.

In this subsection, we will discuss an overview of the defining characteristics of each temperament. As we go along, try to crack your temperament and those of your loved ones.

Let's start.

Sanguine: Extroverted and Stable

Perhaps you know of people who bring sunshine and happiness wherever they go or whoever they are with. They are cheerful, optimistic, and child-like. Their joy radiates in their laughing eyes, genuine smiles, hearty laughter, and loquaciousness or chattiness.

Their good vibes are contagious. Being with them feels light as air. Their giggles and stories are like whistling wind.

The downside is that their chirpiness and positivity may make some people perceive them to be shallow and naïve. Their comfort in their own skin, talkativeness, and being in the limelight may also make them seem big-headed and self-centered.

At their best though, they promote harmony, cooperation, teamwork, and goodwill. They are natural coaches, mentors, counselors, and teachers.

Do you know a person who is like this? Or perhaps you yourself are like this? These descriptions characterize a sanguine temperament.

Choleric: Extroverted and Unstable

Similar with sanguine, people with choleric temperament tend to be extroverted by nature. The difference is that they are less stable versus sanguine personality. Perhaps you know of some individuals who cannot seem to stay still in one place, which seems to always be active and on the go, always needing to be doing something. They are restless, lively, sparkling with energy, and abuzz with activities.

Their element is the roaring fire. Their season is summer when the sun can get scorching hot. They have a fire in their bellies, and they move as if the ground is made of burning coals.

The downside is that their active and overflowing energy can be construed as being fidgety or dominant and bossy. Their strong will and confidence can make them seem cold and intimidating.

The key is to encourage them to unleash, harness, and fulfill their potential as natural leaders, entrepreneurs, and go-getters.

Melancholic: Introverted and Unstable

Melancholic is another unstable temperament, alongside choleric. Individuals with melancholic temperament tend to be introverted too. True to their name, melancholic individuals succumb to melancholy, or overthinking and over-analyzing the past. They may beat themselves for their mistakes and shortcomings. And it's not just about the past, as they are also anxious about the future.

Melancholic may appear to be tough on the outside but are actually quaky and shaky inside. In this sense, they are like their element that is earth. Don't be fooled by their hard, rough, and rigid exterior, because at their core is a magma of thoughts and emotions that may quake the surface from time to time, and may even erupt like a volcano when left uncontrolled.

Their season is autumn or fall, as their thoughts and feelings are like leaves that fall all over the place, cluttering their inner world, sometimes even blowing out into their outer world.

The upside is that melancholic persons are good thinkers, analysts, and planners. At their best, they can think of different possibilities, using what they have learned from the past.

The key is to provide as much as possible a stable environment for melancholic persons to thrive. It is also good to lend a listening and empathic ear to them to listen to their woes and thoughts and emotions, but not too much to the point of co-rumination that may feed their natural tendency to a downward spiral to extreme melancholy and even depression.

Phlegmatic: Introverted and Stable

The last of the temperaments is the most relaxed and chill one. Perhaps you know of persons who are passive and calm, even in dire situations. They are the polar opposites of choleric persons.

Their element is water because they go with the flow. Their season is winter, the most hygge and homey season of all, which is a fitting description to this temperament. The downside is that they can get lazy, lax, and stagnant.

At their best though, they display an admirable grace under pressure that makes people respect them. They may also exude a mature and wise aura, a quiet but nonetheless authoritative presence, someone that people can look up to and listen to.

Temperaments: Putting Them All Together

Each person is a unique mixture of personality traits and temperaments. When it comes to temperament, the typical case is that a person has a primary temperament and a secondary one.

For instance, a person can be primarily phlegmatic, and secondarily a melancholic. This person is a strongly introverted one, and she is balancing her emotional stability depending on situations and persons. Hence, while she is relaxed most times, she is actually thinking about a lot of things deep inside, both about the past and the future.

Another example, a person can be equally choleric and melancholic. This person is quite unstable, and he is balancing his introversion and extroversion depending on what the situation calls for. Restless and anxious, he may direct his energy to the outer world sometimes, managing systems and leading people, but at other times, he may direct it inward and be like thinking and analyzing human machine.

Again, it pays to think of temperament as a spectrum instead of boxes. Real life is more fluid and less clear-cut, and we need to allow room for people to slide across the spectrum.

With the knowledge of how to detect and describe the personalities and temperaments of people, we can gain a deeper understanding, appreciation, and respect for people we deal with on a daily basis.

We learn to cut people some slack and give them benefit of the doubt. We also show interest in them, and this gives them permission to go ahead and be their best selves. In the process, we also give ourselves permission to do the same.

15 - How Do We Use Our Understanding of People to Good Use?

"I am the master of my fate, I am the captain of my soul."

— Invictus, poem by William Ernest Henley

When studying people, we always have to look at the totality. Specifically, we must factor in the following aspects:

- The verbal aspect or what they say,

- Their choice of words,

- How they say it or their pitch and tone of voice,

- Their silence or what they leave unsaid or hanging in the air that prompts us to read between the lines,

- Their non-verbal or what they do, whether they are conscious of these movements or not,

- The disconnect and dissonance between their verbal language and body language including facial expressions,

- Their personal background such as culture, upbringing, personality, and temperament,

- The situation or context, and

- Your gut feel or take on the situation, including how the person makes you feel.

Taking into consideration all these factors, including our own biases and impressions, can help us arrive at a more accurate understanding of people. With enough practice, this exercise can be a more intuitive and automatic thing. It can be second nature to you, and you become more sensitive to people's messages, both explicit and subtle ones.

However, with all these things to watch out for, it is easy to miss the point of studying people. We study people not to judge, but to understand them, and lend help and support when needed. Support can be in the form of just listening and being present, although sometimes, we can help them feel and point them to more positive thoughts and brighter direction.

We can do reverse psychology in cases like this. For example, when dealing with a choleric and turbulent friend who is experiencing a down period, it may be good to challenge them to rise above their situation. Their go-getter attitude and perfectionism may respond well to the challenge.

Or perhaps you have a sad friend. When dealing with a sad person, people usually do things to lighten the person's mood or make the person happy. People ask what they can do to make their feelings better. But wouldn't it be nice if people don't need to ask, but just simply know and do things to make the person feel better? This is when being observant comes in.

We can even apply our keen understanding of human condition to improve ourselves. We know that internal states get manifested in the outer world in one way or another. Simply put, input produces output. But can tweaking the output change the input? It may be a long haul, but it is possible.

We often here of the catchphrase: "Fake it until you make it."

When you feel a lack of confidence, just act confident until you actually feel confident. Walk with a straight back and look people in the eye. When experiencing jitters before a presentation or before speaking or performing in public, jump and move around to release tension, then take deep breaths with eyes closed to slow down your heartbeat and your nerves. You can even recite mantras if you are into that.

If you want to appear more authoritative, practice lowering your voice to modulate your pitch, especially if you tend to speak in a high pitch when excited or when tensed.

When you feel sad and down, move your facial muscles around to tell your brain to stop sulking and brooding. Practice smiling in front of a mirror. Brush your teeth or gurgle. Chew a gum. Talk to a close friend.

Ask a friend to tell you a good joke. Watch cat videos or play with your dog or do whatever makes you feel a warm and fuzzy feeling inside that you can't help but smile. Do whatever works for you. The point is to just move your facial muscles, and perhaps your mood can lighten up too.

When you feel angry, take deep breaths before speaking or sending an angry message. Anger passes, but words cannot be taken back. Unclench and soften your jaw, relax your fists, and part your lips to prevent your teeth from grinding. Release the tensions from your muscles, and you may find anger passing too.

15 - HOW DO WE USE OUR UNDERSTANDING OF PEOPLE TO GOOD USE?

When you feel happy, share the happiness with other people. Send out good vibes to the world. Smile with your eyes, or smile like models do. Who knows? You may encounter people who badly need these uplifting body languages.

As we understand and improve ourselves, we can also gain an understanding of other people, and we may even inspire them to improve themselves.

At the same time, as we understand other people, we learn to appreciate them, and we also realize some things about ourselves that we may not have considered before.

As novelist Dick Wittenborn said, we are the sum of all the people we have ever encountered, met, and interacted with. Community changes us, and we change the community. With a keen and kind understanding, we can direct these changes toward the good and the positive.

16 - Conclusion

Thank you again for buying this book.

I hope this book was able to help you acknowledge and appreciate the complex, multi-faceted, and ever-changing nature of people like you and me. And aside from acknowledgment, I hope this book also inspired you to treat the people around you with sensitivity, understanding, tact, and thoughtfulness.

Remember too, that as you analyze other people, they may also be analyzing you. Hopefully, you were able to get something from this book that could help you become a good person and the best person that you can be.

Best of luck!

Thank You

As we reach the end of this book, I want to say thanks for reading this book.

I want to get this information out to as many people as possible. If you found this book helpful, I would greatly appreciate you leaving me a review. This helps others find the book as well.

Disclaimer

This document is geared towards providing exact and reliable information in regards to the topic and issue covered. The publication is sold on the idea that the publisher is not required to render an accounting, officially permitted, or otherwise, qualified services. If advice is necessary, legal, financial, medical or professional, a practiced individual in the profession should be ordered.

This information is not presented by a financial or medical practitioner and is for entertainment, educational and informational purposes only. The content is not intended as a substitute for professional medical advice, diagnosis, or treatment. Always seek the advice of your physician or other qualified health care provider with any questions you may have regarding a medical condition. Never disregard professional medical advice or delay in seeking it because of something you have read.

The information provided herein is stated to be truthful and consistent, in that any liability, in terms of inattention or otherwise, by any usage or abuse of any policies, processes, or directions contained within is the solitary and utter responsibility of the recipient reader. Under no circumstances will any legal responsibility or blame be held against the publisher for any reparation, damages, or monetary loss due to the information herein, either directly or indirectly.

Last Updated: 27.Sep.2017